UNSTUCK

KARIN MIZGALA

MBA, CFP

SHEILA WALKINGTON

BBA, CFP

How to
Get Ahead
Financially

UNSTUCK

And Start
Living the Life
You Want

MONEY
COACHES
CANADA

moneycoachescanada.ca
womensfinanciallearning.ca

Updated version issued in 2017

For current tax and financial information, visit
moneycoachescanada.ca/resources.

*Unstuck: How to Get Ahead Financially
and Start Living the Life You Want*
is published and distributed by
Money Coaches Canada Inc. — 1st edition

Cover and interior design by Jessica Sullivan
Proofreading by Naomi Pauls, Paper Trail Publishing

ISBN: 978-0-9917054-0-5

PUBLISHER
Money Coaches Canada Inc.
#720-999 West Broadway
Vancouver, BC
V5Z 1K5
moneycoachescanada.ca

ACKNOWLEDGEMENTS

WE WOULD LIKE to thank everyone who has inspired and encouraged us with their enthusiasm and support for our book and for the evolution of Money Coaches Canada.

A Special Thanks to:

OUR CLIENTS, STUDENTS AND READERS: Thank you for sharing your stories, hopes, dreams, worries and desires with us. We are honoured by your trust and confidence in us.

OUR COACHES: Melanie Buffel, Annie Kvick, Tom Feigs, Christine White, Leslie Gardner, Sabine Lay, Karen Richardson, Noel D'Souza, Kathryn Mandelcorn, Alison Stafford, Charmaine Huber, Barbara Knoblach, Anthony Larsen, Janet Gray, Anne Perrault, Sandra Mann, Steve Bridge, Christine Williston, Liisa Tatem, and Nick Boland.

OUR BOOK TEAM: Gillian Shaw, Kim Lear, Jessica Sullivan and Alison Stafford.

OUR MENTORS AND SUPPORTERS: Wayne Gibson, Laurie Winters, Sarah MacGregor, Tracy Theemes, Kamal Basra, Lynne Twist, Juliet Austin, Glennis Deslippe, Maureen Fitzgerald,

Lesley MacDougall, Jayn Steele, Martha Dolan, Steve Walkington, Marion Tennant, Sandra Soroka, John Boon, Debby Wetmore, Tom Bradley, Carrie Gallant, Ruth Kewin, Eva DiCasmirro, Ruth Anne Taves.

OUR PARENTS: Tony & Carol Mizgala and Doug & Connie Walkington.

And mostly,
OUR HUSBANDS: Wayne Melvin and David Flatt for their unfailing love, support and patience.

CONTENTS

PREFACE 1

AWARENESS

1 The Big Secret 7
2 Uncovering Your Money Story 17
3 Making Friends with Your Money 27
4 Money and Relationships 35
5 Help, I Need Somebody! 49
6 Getting What You Really Want 61

KNOWLEDGE/SYSTEMS/TOOLS

7 Your Financial Starting Point 79
8 On Track Money Management System 99
9 Debt: The Good, the Bad and the Ugly 115
10 Invest in Yourself 137
11 Don't Give up on Retirement Yet 167
12 Being Prepared for Emergencies 189
13 Legal Matters 207

TAKE CONSCIOUS ACTION

14 Just Do It 221

RESOURCES 233
INDEX 237

PREFACE

IT WAS JANUARY when a client slipped in the door and sat on the edge of her chair with the guilty air of one who has been called to account for her crimes. The crime? A holiday spending spree—a crime shared by thousands of people who wake up to maxed out credit cards.

But this time, instead of making a minimum payment and hoping a lottery win would bring the nightmare to an end, the woman had decided to seek out a new type of financial help she had read about—a Money Coach. The first step was picking up the phone to make an appointment.

"I almost cancelled," she confessed. "I was too embarrassed to write down how much I owe on my credit cards and I didn't want to admit I'm constantly in my overdraft at the bank."

PART FINANCIAL ADVISOR, part confessor and counselor, as Money Coaches we meet a lot of people who have taken the traditional route to personal financial management and end up feeling like failures. They come to us ashamed, stressed, struggling and reluctant to voice their questions for fear of sounding stupid. Our role isn't to parrot the advice they have no doubt heard over and over:

"Maximize your RSPs, put away six months' pay for emergencies, speed up your mortgage payments." If it was that easy no one would be living in their overdraft and bills would always be paid on time.

The reality is not everyone is born with that financial management gene and some people don't learn about money as they grow up and head out on their own. It's not bad, it's not being stupid, it's just what it is. We start from that point: we don't judge, we don't preach. We're here to help, holding people up, not putting them down.

In our consumer culture we're constantly bombarded with the message that success equals two cars, cell phones, computers, wide-screen TVs, holidays in Hawaii and all the other toys that come with keeping up with the Joneses. Add to that global economic uncertainty, job worries and a cost of living that is going nowhere but up and you have a recipe for financial stress.

Aside from death or serious illness, it's a stress most likely to make us wake up in a cold sweat at night. It's one that brings no end of arguments and dissension in families and relationships.

Platitudes about personal money management can seem like nothing more than lofty goals, impossible to reach. It's no wonder many people are too wrapped in guilt to even face up to their own spending and lack of financial know-how. Instead of feeling optimistic and ready to tackle their finances, they're often ashamed of where they are.

And it's not always about overspending: illness, job losses, divorce, caring for aging relatives—there's a litany of unexpected events that can derail a well-thought-out financial plan and discourage the most conscientious consumer.

IN THIS BOOK we're sharing the experience and advice we've compiled in the 25 years since we started helping people with their money. We're sharing real stories we've heard from clients, although we've changed their names to protect their privacy.

When we started our careers as financial planners selling mutual funds and insurance, we were very successful but we felt something was missing. In spite of being well-paid, educated professionals, our clients felt stuck and were worried they weren't getting ahead financially. We realized they needed more than what we could offer under the traditional financial planning model.

It wasn't enough for us to manage their investments—they needed help with the basics—how to manage their cash flow, get out of debt and cope with transitions—like changing jobs, starting families, launching businesses, buying a house, getting married, being suddenly single, or making the shift to retirement.

They needed someone who could teach them to take control of their own finances. It wasn't just about balancing their books; it was about finding balance in their lives and getting control over money, instead of having money control them. Money coaching isn't about spouting platitudes. It's about creating a framework in which you take control of your finances and feel inspired and motivated rather than judged.

We get the questions people may not want to ask their banker or investment advisor for fear of looking stupid. We hear the confessions of people who are struggling, who feel shame because they think they are the only ones not measuring up to society's message about success.

It's time to break that taboo. If you feel overwhelmed, anxious or stuck financially, you're not alone and there is hope. We have successfully helped our clients achieve financial security and peace of mind using the tools, resources and strategies we will share with you over the coming chapters.

WE HAVE DIVIDED our book into three sections which address both the psychological and technical aspects of money to help you uncover and overcome what's blocking you from feeling good about your money.

SECTION 1: Awareness You will become more aware of your relationship to money, you will learn how to overcome your blocks and fears around money and you will have a clearer picture of what life and financial success means to you.

SECTION 2: Knowledge/Systems/Tools You will learn strategies and techniques for effective money management, including how best to manage your cash flow, how much you need to retire, what investments to choose, whether to pay down the mortgage or invest in an RSP. You will also learn how to manage money through times of transition and change.

SECTION 3: Take Conscious Action You will learn how to take meaningful and conscious steps to personal happiness and financial success.

For additional resources and annual updates on tax and financial information, please visit moneycoachescanada.ca/resources.

WE SINCERELY HOPE that through reading this book and using the resources on our website, you can begin to imagine a life where money is a source of support, peace and true freedom for you and your family.

Karin and Sheila

AWARENESS

▸ 1 ◂

||||||||||||||||||||||||

THE
BIG SECRET

Money is a singular thing. It ranks with love as man's greatest
source of joy. And with death as his greatest source of anxiety.
JOHN KENNETH GALBRAITH

MONEY, MONEY, MONEY—We spend an amazing amount of
time, energy and emotions around money—loving it, hating
it, worrying about it, being frustrated or depressed by it.

Money is one of the biggest factors in our life and most of
us feel terrible about it. We avoid dealing with it, we worry
about losing it, we fight about it, we feel guilty about it, and
we stress and obsess about it.

We can easily feel overwhelmed by debts, the myriad of
investment choices, the general economy, job security, and
pressing retirement decisions. With time pressures and other
life commitments, it's no wonder we avoid thinking about or
dealing with our money.

So we spend more money than we should, we put money
in investments we don't really understand, we buy insurance
we don't need and we pay higher fees for financial products
than necessary.

Deep down we know that something is just not right, but
we typically manage to suppress our worries about money and
carry on in avoidance mode until a crisis hits. We experience a

7

period of unemployment, a divorce, the death of the spouse or unmanageable debts and then the stress really hits.

Money seems to be the killjoy that throws cold water on our hopes, dreams and desires. How often do you think: "If only I had more money, I could…"

However, the truth is there are financial concerns and anxieties at every income level. More money is simply not the answer no matter how tempting that is to believe. Even winning the lotto, cashing in your stock options or inheriting a fortune can prove to be extremely stressful.

A FEW MONTHS AGO a woman came into our office. We were a bit taken aback as she was shabbily dressed and her hair was disheveled. Honestly, we wondered if she had the wrong office.

Turns out she was worth $12 million. But the real kicker was that she was worried she didn't have enough money and would end up as a bag lady living on the streets. How can this be?

Although her case is an extreme example, most of us suffer in some way when it comes to money. Where is the next dollar going to come from? How am I going to pay off the Visa bill? Will I have enough for retirement?

SO WHAT IS IT? Why do so many of us feel that in spite of making good money and not being extravagant we continue to be behind the eight-ball financially?

In her book, *The Soul of Money*, Lynne Twist describes money as "the most universally motivating, mischievous, miraculous, maligned, and misunderstood part of contemporary life." We agree completely.

We're living in an environment where it's almost impossible not to feel pressured to keep up with society's image of success while not overextending ourselves financially. What were once considered wants have now become needs. And with easy access to inexpensive credit and little stigma attached to being in debt, we have a surefire recipe for financial strain.

To make matters worse, the debt culture we've created is starting to show cracks, with extremely high levels of personal and government debt adding more worry and uncertainty on a global level without any easy solutions in sight.

A CLIENT we'll call Janet shared a dilemma that's all too common. To outsiders, it looked like she should have no money worries—she was a well-educated and savvy professional and she was making $60,000 a year after taxes, an income not much below the median after-tax income for Canadian families. And with no partner or family to support, that was seemingly more than enough to ensure Janet could enjoy a comfortable lifestyle.

The problem for Janet could be summed up as the 'keeping up with the Joneses' syndrome, something that can strike us all, whether it's looking at the neighbour's new car with envy, moving to a bigger home to meet family expectations or joining friends on costly vacations that are beyond our means.

Janet's friends all made more money than she did and it left her with the sense that she was somehow inadequate because she couldn't match their spending. In trying to keep up with the travel and other expensive extras her friends could afford, Janet was living beyond her means.

Janet talked about her fear of being judged. She felt ashamed because she wasn't further along financially and she feared in the future she would be even worse off. Janet knew reality would eventually catch up with her and that was causing her great anxiety. It had such a debilitating effect that she almost gave up trying to sort out her finances. She was convinced the problem was her, that she wasn't good at this money stuff.

What it really came down to was her feeling of self-worth. If she failed to keep pace spending-wise with her friends, she felt she was a failure. What a sad commentary on the societal and personal pressures we put ourselves under. It wasn't until Janet took control of her spending and discovered satisfaction in meeting her own financial goals, not trying to keep up with others, that she was able to relax about money and enjoy her financial self-sufficiency.

Money woes can put relationships in peril. While Janet only had to worry about herself, when it comes to couples and money that unease over personal finances is compounded. For the first time in history a lot of women are making more money than their husbands or partners and that's wreaking havoc with relationships where individuals are locked into traditional ideas about who the major income earner should be. On the one hand women want to be independent but for some that's juxtaposed with the feeling that it would be nice to have a partner shouldering the lion's share of the bills.

IT'S A SHIFTING landscape and money is still the last taboo. It's an emotionally charged topic for couples and one it can seem safer to avoid. However, that's a recipe for disaster for your financial and personal relationship. Talking helps you to sort it out. You could find you're both operating out of some ancient belief system, or the values that you have around money are different from your partner's.

In the work we do with clients, we spend as much time listening to them tell us about the guilt, the shame, the worry and the fears they have around money as we do talking about the numbers. Clients share secrets they'd never confess to their banker. For some of them, meeting with a Money Coach is like therapy, they spill their innermost anxieties and financial faux pas they are afraid to tell anyone else.

ONE CLIENT had a large family inheritance but was overwhelmed with a sense of responsibility to 'do the right thing' with the money. Her mother died and left her $500,000, a

sum that should have considerably brightened her financial outlook. But instead of enjoying the inheritance she was
trapped by indecision, afraid to make any move with the
money in case it was the wrong one.

Her dilemma had its roots in her relationship with money.
The relationship had never matured from when she was a
child and her parents took care of all the decisions. She didn't
know how to manage money and the prospect of dealing
with the $500,000 inheritance was daunting.

Having a financial professional take over her parents' role
and simply tell her what to do wasn't the solution. Instead, in
our coaching sessions she was able to voice her fears as they
related to money. Financial advisors had intimidated her and
in talking to them, she felt like a child again, not wanting to
admit everything they said was over her head.

It wasn't just that indecision was preventing her from
making major decisions, like whether or not she should buy
a home; it was also putting the brakes on other areas of her
life. Once she took control of her financial issues, it proved a
catalyst that let her move forward with her life, including her
career, which seemed to be frozen in the general anxiety that
was enveloping her over money. She was spinning her wheels,
she couldn't move forward until she dealt with the management of her money.

THESE ARE THE kinds of stories we hear all the time and no
doubt you have your own money stories. If you keep those
hidden within you, locked away so you don't even have to
admit them to yourself, it's like trying to cap a volcano that
sooner or later will erupt.

There are influences you may not even recognize as being
part of your financial story but most likely they'll show up
somewhere in how you relate to money. All too often it is
these factors that limit your ability to be successful with
money and, more importantly, with your life.

SEVEN STAGES OF FINANCIAL WELL-BEING

7 FINANCIAL
FULFILLMENT

6 FINANCIAL
FREEDOM

5 FINANCIAL
SECURITY

4 FINANCIAL
STABILITY

3 FINANCIAL
AWARENESS

2 FINANCIAL
AVOIDANCE

1 FINANCIAL
CHAOS

7 Emotions: I have enough, generosity, sharing
Behaviours: Charitable giving, setting up foundations, involved in humanitarian projects, giving back (time and money)
Financial Status: Money is no object and a non-issue, "I have everything I need and more," knowledge, wealth allocation, giving back (time and money)

6 Emotions: Sense of achievement, what's next? life purpose issues, fear of loss, do I really have enough?
Behaviours: Retirement, downsizing, volunteer work, living elsewhere, travel
Financial Status: Achieved financial independence, focus on personal enjoyment

5 Emotions: Confidence, control, openness
Behaviours: Planning for the future, considering life choices and assessing options
Financial Status: Provided for unexpecteds: estate plan, insurance up to date, children's education saved for, savings plan maximized, minimal & controlled debt

4 Emotions: Relief, sense of accomplishment, cautiously optimistic
Behaviours: Looking for reassurance, seeking information, getting organized
Financial Status: Have advisor or a plan for savings, debt under control, living within means, building assets (RSPs, home), good money management skills

3 Emotions: Curiosity, trepidation, willingness
Behaviours: Ready to take charge and change habits
Financial Status: Developing consciousness of need for a plan, often prompted by excessive debt, external event (job, divorce), ready to be educated and to take charge

2 Emotions: Overwhelm, confusion, insecurity, frustration
Behaviours: Paralysis, not sure where to turn, head in the sand
Financial Status: Random savings, no advisor, disorganized finances, bank accounts in various places, little financial control and knowledge

1 Emotions: Fear, guilt, shame
Behaviours: Avoiding, abdicating, overspending, family conflicts
Financial Status: No savings, taxes not done, bills unpaid, mail unopened, abdicate to parent or spouse

Seven Stages of Financial Well-Being

Attaining financial well-being is a process; it's not an overnight transformation from fiscal imprudence to fiscal prudence. There are seven stages in this process and while you may feel like you're at the bottom of the pyramid, stuck in financial chaos, there is hope.

You can gradually move up the pyramid, getting through the phase of financial avoidance until you finally reach the point at which you're ready to begin learning: financial awareness. From there it's not such a steep climb to achieve financial stability, then financial security and on to financial freedom and ultimately to the top of the pyramid, financial fulfillment.

At each stage along the way there are different emotions, behaviours and financial realities that you may experience. Where do you think you fit now? Where do you want to be in one year, five years, 10 years?

By having more awareness and understanding of your money story and the positive and negative influences that have affected your relationship to money, you'll be in a better position to engage more proactively with your finances and far more likely to take the steps you need to develop habits and implement strategies that will build financial ease.

While many of your longstanding habits and worries about money may not dissolve overnight, the process of becoming honest with yourself and being curious about the role money has played in your life is crucial in setting the stage to learn new ways to grow your financial net worth.

So What's the Big Secret to Financial Success that No One Is Telling You?

There isn't one. In reality, money isn't all that complicated or interesting—even for financial educators and Money Coaches like us. It certainly doesn't deserve all the press it gets—either positive or negative. Don't get us wrong, there's certainly nothing wrong with enjoying what money has to offer—the freedom it gives you to live the life you want, the ability to care for your family and to contribute to causes you believe in.

But in our experience, true financial freedom isn't as much about the dollars and cents as it is about knowing what's important to you and aligning the way you make and manage money with your values, passions and life purpose.

A STUDY was done 20 years ago on how people got rich. There were 1,500 participants and 80% of the participants said that they would go out and make enough money so they could quit and then do what they really wanted to do. The remaining 20% said they'd do what they loved and worry about the money later. Out of the 1,500, 101 became millionaires and only one of those millionaires was from the group that just wanted to make money.

So by focusing on living a happier, more fulfilling life, you'll likely end up making more money anyway. However the most important take-away is that financial well-being is a function of how well you engage with and manage your money, not the amount of money you have.

It's so easy to fall into the trap of "when I have the money I will do this, feel this, and be this." However, unless you're able to define what enough means to you, it's very easy to get caught in a wheel of continually striving and chasing after something that's ever-elusive and unattainable.

We have to begin questioning the conventional wisdom of acquiring and accumulating beyond what we truly need. Gandhi said it beautifully: *"The world has enough for our need but not for our greed."*

So the first step in financial self-sufficiency is to ask yourself: "How much do I really *need* to live a comfortable, balanced and meaningful life now and in the future?" This certainly doesn't mean deprivation and poverty, but it does mean being aware of how money flows through your life and making conscious and informed choices about how you make, manage and invest your money.

It also means taking responsibility for your personal finances, aligning your financial life with your values and beliefs and realizing your self-worth isn't based on how much money you have.

Spiritual leader Maharishi Mahesh Yogi spoke of money as a "medium of transformation." What's so reassuring about this phrase is that it both captures the potential that money has and at the same time it puts money in its proper place. Money is simply a medium, not an end in itself.

It's certainly not easy to maintain this higher-level perspective while in the midst of our frenzied lifestyle and consumer culture. But the more awareness you have about the role money plays in your life, the more you can clear any blocks you have around your relationship to it. And the more comfortable you are with the mechanics of money, the quicker you will experience how money can be a medium of transformation.

What this allows you to do on a practical level is to look at the numbers without fear, to plan for the future with confidence and to enjoy what money has to offer without guilt. It means you can get off the treadmill of working harder yet feeling further behind and start owning your ability to make wise, life-affirming choices.

Taking control of your finances can be challenging, but the rewards of financial peace of mind and security are well worth your efforts. In the coming chapters, we'll help you meet those challenges by giving you the tools, tips and resources you need to bring more joy and ease into your financial life—one step at a time.

▸ 2 ◂

||||||||||||||||||||||||||

UNCOVERING
YOUR
MONEY STORY

Money is the opposite of the weather.
Nobody talks about it,
but everybody does something about it.
REBECCA JOHNSON

EVERY YEAR BOB AND MAGGIE would come into our office for a review meeting and immediately the conversation turned to how soon their portfolio would be large enough so they could retire. Bob hated his job and all he could think of was the date that he could break free. The sad thing was that he was only 43 years old and no matter how we crunched the numbers, retirement was still at least 15 years away.

Because Bob saw money as his only route to freedom, he was furious when his portfolio went down and all too eager to invest in very high-risk investments when the markets did well. Needless to say Bob wasn't an easy client to work with, but mostly it was disheartening to see how his rigid belief system about money trapped him in a cycle of irrational decision making and unhappiness. Unfortunately, Bob was so entrenched in his belief that building a large nest egg was the only solution to his unhappiness that he never allowed himself to consider other options.

Bob certainly isn't alone in making decisions that tie money directly to happiness but what is the real link between the two?

Money and Happiness

Lara Aknin is a doctoral student working with Dr. Michael Norton, assistant professor at Harvard Business School, and Dr. Elizabeth Dunn, professor of psychology at the University of British Columbia. They are part of a growing body of researchers examining the links between money and happiness.

"Money is only one factor that influences happiness," Aknin says. "Work in the fields of social and positive psychology, shows that personal relationships, religious beliefs, exercise, feelings of gratitude, random acts of kindness, as well as higher income, can all affect our sense of well-being."

According to their research, "a striking inconsistency surrounds the relationship between money and happiness." It suggests that people "engage in behaviours designed to increase or maintain their wealth because they overestimate the impact that income has on well-being."

This link between money and happiness is often learned and reinforced through the messages we get from our families, workplaces and the media, so it's hard not to adopt these same beliefs and be influenced by them—most likely unconsciously. You probably haven't had many opportunities in your life to step back and consider how you make financial decisions, so it's possible you're making choices that actually sabotage your unique definition of true happiness and fulfillment without really being aware of it.

We see the madness in the irrational feelings people have about money that make otherwise rational adults behave very foolishly. Symptoms can include working harder than is healthy, overspending, going into excessive debt, buying high and selling low in the markets out of panic, incessantly watching our stock portfolio, obsessing about the financial news and lying to our spouses or business partners. It can be equating one's self-worth with net worth. It may be not saving or planning for the future, not living one's dreams or pursuing one's goals or not having a sense of purpose. The results are all too often depression, anxiety, fear, anger, drug and alcohol abuse and other self-destructive behaviours.

Spencer Sherman, author of the *The Cure for Money Madness*, claims that the number one factor in achieving true, joyful and fulfilling financial freedom isn't budgeting and financial know-how or how much you earn—it's transforming your inner relationship to money.

Without a healthy emotional relationship to our money—and seeing how our finances fit into a balanced and purposeful life—we're going to stay stuck in the madness. To break the cycle of financial distress, the underlying emotional foundations surrounding our beliefs about money must be considered. It's only then that we'll be free to enjoy the money we make and the things that we own without stress or guilt.

Developing a Healthy Relationship with Money

Most people stress about money. For some, it's about making ends meet or family conflicts; for others it's about long-term financial security, being taken advantage of, or the ups and downs in the stock market. Whatever your stress, you can improve your relationship with money by becoming more aware of what's blocking you from financial peace and taking the steps to set yourself free.

Developing a healthy relationship to money isn't a get-rich-quick scheme. It takes commitment, time, energy and discipline, but if you remember that money is simply a tool to help you live the life you want, the rewards are well worth it.

In a healthy relationship with money, your money supports you to live a satisfying, fulfilling and meaningful life, and you in turn, respect your money enough to learn how it works, to be honest with where you stand with it, and to do the best you can with it.

To assess where you stand with money now, start by asking yourself these questions:

How do I know if my relationship with money is healthy?

Begin by examining your beliefs and thoughts about money and reflect on your experience with money both past and present. How did your parents handle money? Was it a source of stress in your family when you were growing up? Do you spend money to make yourself feel better? Are you satisfied with the amount of money you have? Do you avoid opening your bills? Are you a shopaholic? Do you put off making financial decisions and taking control of your money?

Is my money working for me or am I working for it?

It's tempting to think that more money will solve your problems, but having more doesn't guarantee a better relationship with money or increased happiness. Some 70% of lottery winners blow their winnings within a few years and end up where they started—or worse. Studies have shown that as long as a person has enough money for his or her basic needs, more money doesn't necessarily bring greater happiness.

In fact, it can add to your stress, especially if you fall into the keeping up with the Joneses trap. A study led by Harvard University post-doctoral researcher Jordi Quoidbach, "Money Giveth, Money Taketh Away: The Dual Effect of Wealth on Happiness," found that even though money allows people to buy more, it can dampen their ability to savour everyday positive emotions and experiences.

By asking yourself the question "If money were no object, what would I do with my life?" you can free up your imagination to dream and remember what really matters to you. It's amazing how easy it is to lose sight of your life purpose when you're using all of life's energy to maintain the wheel of consumption.

How can I live the life that I want?

Are you waiting for financial security before living a more meaningful life? Are you allocating time or money to causes that you believe in?

If you're waiting to reach some magic number in your bank account or to be debt-free before you start living the life you want, you're probably giving money way too much hold over your life. While it's important to pay the bills and to be financially responsible, a healthy relationship to money comes from using money to support your dreams and goals, not as an end in itself. It's important to be clear about what you want your life to look like, to do what you can to get your financial house in order and align your money with your life.

Did I inherit my attitude towards handling money from my parents?

How did your parents handle money? Were they extravagant spenders or excessive savers? What messages did you pick up about money as a child? Chances are the impact of these messages is buried pretty deep and could be influencing the way you handle money today. You might have adopted the same dysfunctional behaviours and beliefs as your parents or you might have swung to the other extreme—spending recklessly to counteract the penny-pinching attitude you grew up with. The key to freeing yourself from the stresses of past conditioning is to bring these memories to a level of awareness and to take a good hard look at how they may be affecting your relationship to money today.

THIS STORY about our client Amy illustrates how parents can inadvertently send their children very different messages.

The lessons Amy learned from her father were very direct:
"My first allowance was five pennies. One penny had to go to helping someone else and the other four were for me. Every Sunday, when Dad gave me my allowance I had to account for what I had done with the previous week's pennies. He taught me to use my money to help others and to help myself and he taught me to plan for the future—he had me investing in RSPs and doing my own taxes when I was 18."

The lessons Amy learned from her mother were indirect:
"My mother used money as an excuse for not taking control of her life. She used to say: "If I had the money, I would leave your father, get my own apartment and travel." Like many women of her generation, she felt powerless in her marriage. I spent my teenage years trying to prove that she had the power to change her life, but her argument against me often came back to money. I learned that I never wanted to feel powerless, and that maintaining financial control of my life would afford me precious choices."

How well do I communicate?
If you have had fights with your spouse about money, you know how stressful and destructive they can be to a relationship. In fact, money issues are considered to be one of the major causes of divorce. As difficult as it is to talk about money matters, communication is essential in working through financial woes. Set aside a specific time to talk about money concerns and involve a third party if the discussions get too emotionally heated. As Money Coaches we often fill that role, helping partners focus on mutual goals, to be clear about what their needs are and to avoid the blame game. And be patient in those discussions—your spouse is probably struggling with as many mixed messages about money as you are.

Am I ready to learn?

How many times have you met with a financial advisor, nodded your head, but really had no idea what was being said? The financial and investment world is increasingly complex and if you don't understand the language of money, you can be left feeling very vulnerable and uneasy. Even if you work with an advisor you trust, the only way to truly overcome this anxiety is to educate yourself about money. Take a money course, read a book on financial planning or look for an advisor who focuses on financial education. You don't have to become a real estate guru or an expert on the stock market, but make sure you are *delegating, not abdicating* responsibility for your finances.

Am I drowning in debt?

Debt limits your options, simple as that. THE MORE DEBT YOU HAVE, THE LESS CONTROL YOU HAVE OVER YOUR LIFE AND YOUR CHOICES. Nothing causes more stress than working at a job you don't like just to make your monthly credit card payments. While it may be hard to avoid incurring some debt (home ownership for instance), make sure you have a plan for repaying the debt as quickly as possible. Try to resist the convenience and reward incentives of credit cards. You might get a free trip to New York but the real cost could be your overall financial well-being.

Am I living within my means?

According to Statistics Canada, more than 50% of Canadians spend more than they earn. No wonder we're stressed about money! The most important financial principle is to figure out how much money you need for your current lifestyle and how much you need to save for future goals and dreams. Then, find out how much income you earn after taxes and deductions. If you spend more than you earn and have nothing left over for savings, take a hard look at your expenses or find a way to make more money. There's no easy solution here, just a cold, hard look at the financial numbers.

Am I worrying too much about money?

Many of us are filled with anxiety, fear and stress over the turbulent financial markets, the political and economic turmoil and the impact on our own financial situation. Some of that fear is justified—times are challenging—but much of what we worry about is beyond our control. Money, no matter how much we have, can never be a complete proxy for safety and security and there are no absolute guarantees with any financial strategy.

What we can control is how we evaluate and respond to outside influences. Since we're susceptible to emotional reactions during times of stress or euphoria, it helps to create a well-thought-through financial plan that you can stick to in both good times and bad. A plan helps restore common sense and rational thinking that will allow you to ride through economic and market storms without falling into a destructive emotional reaction.

Do I have a good handle on my money now?

Here's a five-point checklist to see where you stand:

	Yes	No
1. I have completed a Net Worth statement: I've added up the value of everything I own (my assets) and subtracted what I owe (liabilities) to come up with my net worth.	☐	☐
2. I manage my cash flow well, and I'm comfortable that I'm not spending more than I earn.	☐	☐

	Yes	No

3. I have a *Spending and Savings Plan* so I know money is there to pay the bills when they come due and I can make choices about whether it's more important to save for a designer dress or if I'd rather put that money towards a ski trip. ☐ ☐

4. I have built up a good credit history and I pay off my credit card in full every month so I'm not paying high-interest rates to fund buying that is beyond my means. ☐ ☐

5. I have an investment and retirement plan which I review regularly and I seek professional advice because it's worse to remain in ignorance than to worry about asking questions for fear of looking dumb. ☐ ☐

If you have answered yes to most of these questions, you're on your way.
You have a handle on your finances and you're aware of the key issues that can make a difference between financial security and not sleeping at night because you're worried about paying the bills.

If you didn't answer yes to all of these questions or to any of them, don't be too hard on yourself, you're not alone.
But it is time to take control. In this book we will help you do that, giving you the tools and the information you need to create a plan and a system for managing your money.

▸ 3 ◂

||||||||||||||||||||||||

MAKING FRIENDS
WITH YOUR MONEY

Money makes a good servant, but a bad master.
FRANCIS BACON

HOW WOULD YOU describe your relationship to money? Do you
see money as a trusted, supportive friend, there for you at all
stages of your life? Or is your experience with money more
like a trip to the dentist—you know it's good for you, but oh,
so unpleasant. Maybe you're more like Scarlett O'Hara with
your money—"I'll think about that tomorrow." Or perhaps
your dreams of comfort and ease in retirement are eclipsed
by visions of yourself as a bag lady?

Chances are money is something you don't want to spend
a lot of time thinking about and when you do, it's only
because you're forced to by external events. Even though you
might tell yourself that you *should* get a better handle on
your money, it usually takes a significant life event or crisis—
job loss, divorce, retirement—to bring money issues to the
forefront. Unfortunately, because of the emotions brought on
by life changes, this is rarely the best time to make rational
financial decisions.

Why does this happen? Why is it that we avoid giving serious thought to our money until it's forced upon us?

Mostly it comes down to fear—fear that we'll have to face our shortcomings, fear of being judged, fear of having to make hard choices and fear of change.

The Top 10 Common Fears and Obstacles We See:

1. **What-if syndrome** What if it's worse than I thought? What if I don't have enough?
2. **Abdicating responsibility** Someone else can probably manage things better than I can.
3. **Intimidation** I'm too embarrassed to ask questions; everyone knows more than I do.
4. **Mommy and Daddy syndrome** My parents will leave me money. My dad will always bail me out.
5. **Shame** I should have done things differently; I should be farther ahead than I am.
6. **Conflicts with spouse** If we can't agree I'd rather drop it. It's easier not to talk about it.
7. **I wish syndrome** I wish I could win the lottery or receive an inheritance from a long-lost uncle.
8. **Procrastination** I don't have enough money yet; I'll plan when I have more.
9. **Prince Charming syndrome** My husband or husband-to-be will take care of me.
10. **Conflicted values** I shouldn't focus on money; that's what selfish people do.

Do any of these fears and obstacles sound familiar? Most people can pick out several that resonate for them. Add to that our time-strapped lives and just overcoming the hurdle of knowing where to start and it's no wonder people would rather avoid facing up to their money issues.

OUR CLIENT BARBARA had put off dealing with her financial issues as long as possible when she finally sought out money coaching. She is a successful counselor and in our sessions together was able to clearly articulate how she felt as we reviewed her income and expenses. She said she found it hard to breathe and described her anxiety as we tallied her numbers. She talked about her fear of being judged, the worry about facing reality, the shame of not being further along financially and her fear for the future. Fortunately, she felt safe enough to talk about how she was feeling and together we were able to name the fears and bring them to the surface. We could then address them gently and logically. She left with a concrete action plan and she was immensely relieved that she had finally confronted some of her financial demons.

Barbara's story is not uncommon. The fear that keeps us from shining a light on our finances is usually far worse than the reality. As one of our clients told us: *"Doing the work hasn't stressed me out at all. It's NOT doing the work that was really stressing me out."*

Understanding Our Emotions

Understanding how your emotions impact your financial decisions is key to breaking unconscious patterns and unlocking your financial power. The first step is to understand where your emotions, assumptions and baggage come from. Just like your relationships with people, your relationship with money is heavily influenced by those around you. We learn by observing. We observe our parents, our peers and the media. Unfortunately, they aren't always great teachers and the messages we get about money can get ridiculously mixed up. It's up to you to check in with yourself, to turn off the noise about things you *should* be doing and discover what matters to you, not to those around you.

Mixed Messages

We are constantly being bombarded by mixed messages. Here are some of the more common ones—you've probably heard them from family, friends, colleagues, and maybe they're even messages you tell yourself.

MIXED MESSAGE 1: Do as I say, not as I do.

Your parents may or may not have intentionally taught you about money, but without a doubt you learned a lot from them. Whatever you experienced in your family, good and bad, set the stage for the way you relate to money today.

Bring your memories to a level of awareness where you can look at the choices you're making today and assess whether you truly own your actions or if you're reacting to a past that you need to lay to rest.

MIXED MESSAGE 2: Money can't buy happiness, but buying stuff is fun and makes me feel better.

The first part of the message is true. Money can't buy happiness. Research by the University of Pennsylvania suggests happiness is related to your feelings of community engagement, the alignment of your actions with your goals, living and working from your strengths and—believe it or not—to practice. So what about the second part of the message? Does buying stuff make you feel better? Is it fun?

Advertising campaigns and even friends reinforce the pleasures of parting with your hard-earned cash. They tell you: "You'll be happier, safer, healthier, thinner, (fill in your wish here) when you have…"

But picture it, you've bought all the right anti-aging, soul-enlightening, nonfat, memory-boosting, fast-acting, self-cleaning, make-more-time-for-yourself stuff you can afford (and possibly a bit more). Now you're looking at your bank statement; a printout of all the fun you've had. Are you still having fun?

Buying stuff to make yourself feel better is certainly a diversion tactic. But if you think the amusement you get out of it is lasting, you're fooling yourself.

See if you recognize this cycle of fun: I'm stressed. I need to have some fun. I buy things and go places that cost a bit more than I can really afford but I'm worth it. I eventually get my credit card statement, then I see just how much the fun cost me. I'm stressed.

Our culture touts fun as the antidote to stress and unhappiness. But when fun comes back to cause you stress, you need to find a new source of amusement and think about what truly brings you fulfillment. The real antidote to stress is a positive outlook—and a plan.

MIXED MESSAGE 3: Do more. Buy more. Earn more. Relax more. Huh?

It is easy to see why we need to relax, but who can? If you sit still for a moment, it's time you could be doing, buying, experiencing or working. The solution seems to be to do all those things while you relax.

What happened to stretching out on a lawn chair or walking in the park? Now we chill out at the mall. Or we spend $120 on a massage and manicure. Or we shell out $2,500 for an all-inclusive week in Cancun. And don't forget to cram two weeks of work into one before you go! Ahhh.

Shopping, spa treatments and holidays are great (really great) but if you have to spend more than you earn to relax, you're going to stress yourself out. It's basic math: Working your tail off + debt = stress

Do you ever wonder if our culture's newfound passion for expensive relaxation is really just a cover for a communal panic caused by living beyond our means? So let go of the myth that more is more. Most of us don't really need more but we're conditioned to *want more, consume more and expect more.*

When architects and designers design a room for relaxation they work with the less-is-more philosophy. Lose the clutter. Turn off the noise. Take the pressure off. Enjoy living within your means.

MIXED MESSAGE 4: I deserve it.

Deserve what? Do you deserve to be in debt? Do you deserve to be panicked about money? Do you deserve to be a slave to a paycheque? Think about that the next time you want to treat yourself to something you think you deserve but know you can't afford.

You deserve to live your best life. You deserve to feel satisfaction and contentment when you pick up your bank statement. You deserve to achieve your goals. You deserve financial control of your life!

MIXED MESSAGE 5: We're friends, we can talk about anything, except money.

Why is it that we will share the most intimate details of our sex lives but we won't talk about money? Your friends might teach you how to convince your partner it was his idea to renovate the kitchen, but who's sharing secrets about their RSP investments?

It's time to break the silence. We can learn and share and shed financial chains together. Talk to your friends about money. Inquire after their financial health. Let them know they can talk to you about their hopes and fears.

The "I'm Not Good With Money" Trap

Part of the reason it's hard to talk about money is the belief that we're just not good at it. Unfortunately, this can become a vicious cycle and self-fulfilling prophecy. We lack the confidence to engage with our money so we avoid thinking about it and learning about it, and that ultimately leads us right back to avoiding it and feeling intimidated and vulnerable. It's not a good feeling.

Who are you giving your power away to? Is it your spouse, your banker, an investment advisor, your employer? It's so easy to do, and you might be doing it without realizing what's happening or what the implications are.

If money isn't your thing you might never be interested in knowing all the inner workings of the stock market or macro-economic theory. However, you do need to know the basics. Not understanding money is not the same as not understanding cars or home appliances. While you may end up getting taken by your car mechanic or appliance repairman, the worst that could happen is you pay a few bucks more for your repairs. If you completely abdicate responsibility for your finances, your whole well-being may be at stake—clearly a more serious problem.

Claiming Your Financial Power

Even if watching paint dry still seems like a more enjoyable pursuit than dredging up old money wounds or learning basic financial literacy skills, the life you want depends on educating, enlightening and empowering yourself about money. Unfortunately, there are no shortcuts, no magic bullets or hidden secrets.

It does take being open to a mindset shift, a commitment to having a different relationship with money and courage to face some of the demons you may have been trying to avoid.

Try to identify the specific behaviours, beliefs or habits that have been holding you back from feeling successful with money. Then think about how you want to feel about money. What would it look like if you finally were able to see money as a trusted partner instead of something you have to battle against?

Take small, manageable steps towards financial empowerment and be realistic with what you can accomplish at any one time. There's no need to be an expert overnight. If you try to absorb too much new information or take on too many tasks on your financial to-do list, you're more likely to be overwhelmed and abandon your best intentions altogether.

Also remember the road to financial enlightenment is a process and it's easy enough to fall back into negative patterns. Change doesn't always happen immediately so be patient and acknowledge all wins no matter how small they may be. Cross your financial to-do's off your list with delight, savour the joy of having the money in your account *before* your vacation, and burn your mortgage statements when the house is paid off.

While you may be ready to take more responsibility for your financial life, it may be challenging to engage your partner or family in the process. The next chapter looks at the tricky business of money and relationships.

▸ 4 ◂

||||||||||||||||||||||||

MONEY AND RELATIONSHIPS

I don't care too much for money / For money can't buy me love.
BEATLES

MOST OF US don't find money an easy thing to talk about in our culture. It's rarely discussed openly in our families, we don't tell our friends what we earn, we feel uncomfortable negotiating our salary and we often avoid the topic with our partners for fear of rocking the boat.

Somehow our lack of openness about money has become an acceptable norm but unless we challenge that norm and become more comfortable talking about money, it will wield too much power over us and hurt our most important relationships.

Couples and Money

For many couples nothing dampens love and ardour more than the subject of finances. In fact, study after study shows that money problems are the single biggest cause of relationship stress and divorce—with sex and raising kids rounding out the big three. While talking about money can be more difficult and emotionally charged than talking about sex, religion or politics, open dialogue can save a lot of tension and resentments in your relationship.

When stock markets slide and unemployment increases, relationships inevitably suffer. Couples are facing huge challenges right now, because money issues come with very charged emotions. Financial issues threaten our bonds of intimacy and trust and many people lack the skills and the willingness to talk about their finances. We often find distorted childhood perceptions of money can poison even the strongest relationships. One of the biggest problems is lack of openness between partners. And different values, experiences and expectations can result in a rift that is difficult to negotiate around. That's why it can sometimes take an impartial third party, like a therapist, financial advisor or Money Coach to help get negotiations with your partner moving again when you've come to a financial standstill.

Learning to eliminate secrets, lies, and overspending are just a few ways couples can get back on track, increase intimacy, and make their relationship stronger.

It might be difficult to talk about money issues, but hiding from problems and not setting aside time to talk only increases stress. And that stress results in some pretty crazy thinking and behaviour. Under too much stress we lose clarity in thinking and revert to primitive means of dealing with problems: anger—or even worse, suppression of anger—and feelings of inadequacy or resentment or bitterness. This means we're pulled even deeper into money madness which can lead to bad decisions about spending, saving, and investing money.

Let's acknowledge that when it comes to money we're talking about a complex range of issues, many of them shaped by family and social attitudes likely formed long before we even met our partners. These range from spending and savings habits, to a need for security, to risk tolerance, attitudes around debt, planning for the future, and so on. These approaches to money—both positive and negative—are then modified once again with every change in our financial circumstances. Those changes can come with age, children, career shifts, the economic climate, our health, approaching retirement, and the numerous other setbacks or opportunities that life throws our way.

Given the complexity of issues—and the wide range of emotions that accompanies the whole package—it's no wonder we are dealing with a potentially explosive topic. Dealt with properly however there are also great opportunities here for strengthening your partnership and fulfilling your mutual dreams and goals.

SO WHERE do we start? Simple!

STEP 1: Talk, talk, talk.

STEP 2: Listen, listen, listen.

Easy enough, right? Well, okay, maybe not. So let's elaborate a bit so we can put those two simple action steps into something more concrete and workable in your real-life situation.

8 STEPS TO FINANCIAL BLISS FOR COUPLES

1. **Start talking about what is important:** The most likely reason couples fight about money is that they haven't learned to talk openly about money. When the subject does come up it's often the result of a conflict or crisis. Start a dialogue with your partner about your financial goals and values and remember your partner is your ally, not your enemy. You don't have to agree on all your goals, but you do have to acknowledge and appreciate your loved one's dreams and aspirations. Hopefully you'll have some common goals, like retirement, but your individual goals are just as important to your emotional and financial health.

2. **Build a financial plan around your goals:** This process gives you a lot to talk about and the plan itself will guide you both

down the same path. The key to a healthy partnership is communicating clearly about your current financial situation and about your plans for the future.

3. **Spend and save your money to consistently support you both:** That means you know and agree on how much of your money is for things that you both need (rent or mortgage, for instance), how much is for common goals (travel and retirement), and how much you each can use for your individual goals (singing lessons or a new TV).

4. **Stage your goals: You can't do everything at once.** If you only have $200 to put towards your goals each month, you may choose to allocate it all to one goal. Choosing to achieve one thing before another is okay as long as you both know when your turn will come, and you both stick to the plan.

5. **Be a friend, don't overspend:** Don't deprive your spouse by overspending or going into debt. If one person overdoes it, the other has less financial support to do what they want. Don't rely on your spouse to tell you when to stop spending— it just isn't fair to ask your partner to 'play the bad guy.'

6. **Don't hide spending, savings, or feelings:** A strong relationship is based on trust and open communication. Both people in a relationship may not approach money the same way, but you can each learn how the other feels about money by listening. Build your trust and your net worth together.

7. **Joint responsibilities, joint account:** Put both of your paycheques into a joint bank account to cover all major expenses such as rent or mortgage payments, monthly bills, retirement savings, a holiday fund and expenses you incur together. Each partner then gets a personal allowance to spend as they

want—for coffee, clothes, hairstyling, sports gear, hobbies, tech toys and other items on their own personal wish list.

8. **Deal with debt:** This is especially important in times of economic change or uncertainty. Likely no issue divides couples more than this. Attitudes vary widely on debt, and by the time people realize they have a problem the stress levels are already at a crisis point. The result is often denial, feeling guilty or blaming our partner, and fear, anger or resentment, with the problem compounded by bad decisions or band-aid solutions.

Spenders, Savers, Avoiders

It's rare that couples come to see us in perfect agreement over the state of their finances. More often, one is the spender and the other is the saver, which can put personal and financial strain on the relationship. Often the spender is also an avoider who knows they're in a financial predicament but finds it easier to pretend it isn't happening than to actually face up to it.

In some relationships, both individuals may be avoiders. We have worked with couples where one overspends and the other is so afraid of upsetting or angering the spender that both just avoid dealing with the fact they are heading for—at best—considerable downsizing and constraints on their spending if not outright financial ruin.

WE HAVE ONE COUPLE amongst our clients—and they're by no means alone in this practice—where the husband has the financial wherewithal to realize they're spending way more than they make but he keeps digging his head deeper in the sand, mainly because he just doesn't want to upset his wife.

They nod a lot but nothing really changes. They continue to overspend and their income isn't meager—between them they make between $300,000 and $350,000.

Both of them are avoiding dealing with their financial issues and as a result they'll have no choice but to sell their house and downsize. They typically rack up $8,000 a month on credit cards, overspending by $5,000 to $6,000 a month. And their huge mortgage gets bigger as all that excess spending goes first onto their line of credit and then onto their mortgage. Their line of credit is maxed out and the equity in their home is dropping as they shift more debt onto their mortgage.

They're being forced to sell their house yet they're fighting to get their kids into private school. They've never had to rein in their spending and they're not alone. This behaviour is something that is widespread and deeply entrenched in our culture. It seems we can throw ourselves headlong towards financial ruin, yet we're still concerned with the car we drive, the private schools and all the other trappings of the so-called successful life.

IF THIS DESCRIBES you and your relationship, it is time to bring in a third party to diffuse some of that emotion and help halt that headlong rush to financial disaster.

In the case of the overspending couple, the husband who was the saver, not the spender, said he and his wife couldn't talk about their financial situation on their own. It wasn't enough for him to tell her the overspending must end; that message had to come from an independent outsider, in this case a Money Coach.

Such subjects are charged with emotion, and having those discussions with a third party will help to dissolve some of that emotion and inertia. This isn't to sugarcoat financial problems in a relationship. But the first step is admitting the reality of the problem, and in almost every case there is a solution if people are willing to listen and if they're willing to learn how to make good financial decisions.

For the husband and wife who hit the financial wall, the husband had already realized their dilemma, but it was only with the support from a Money Coach that he was able to convince his wife they must change their ways.

AS MONEY COACHES, in our own lives we deal with the same kinds of issues as our clients. In Karin's case, she is, not surprisingly, the financially organized one while her husband before they were married thought nothing of spending $80 on a grocery bag of exotic fruit.

"It took tremendous patience and many, many conversations, some pretty heated, for us to reach a place that we were both comfortable with how to manage our finances together" says Karin.

IT IS DEFINITELY a dance to make it work, but first the partners must be ready to talk about these issues. If you're with someone who is not willing to talk or engage in that dance that leads to a balanced and secure financial future, think again before you rush into marriage or a long-term commitment. If it's too late and you're already committed, seek outside help from a therapist, Money Coach or financial advisor.

Financial professionals and therapists can't wave a wand and magically change a person's behaviour, but financial transformation is possible—and results can be immediate. Many of our clients have told us that they have felt a dramatic sense of relief and excitement the minute they hired us.

Growing Families

There's nothing like becoming a parent to get you thinking about your financial future and the life you want to create as a family. But as well as all the juggling you're already doing with your children, you may also be concerned about getting by on one salary, going back to work, managing your money to allow you to meet your goals and saving for your child's education. And when you get overwhelmed by these worries—and most parents do—you tend to put them on the back burner, planning to focus on them when you're less tired, when you have more time or more money.

Fortunately, there are some simple and practical ways to make sure you are doing the best you can with your family finances. Here are a few tips and resources to get you started:

1. Make sure you are on the same page as your spouse about your life goals and financial priorities—what do you want your life and lifestyle to look like?
2. Set aside a dedicated time to have financial conversations with your spouse to review and to stay on track with your goals.
3. Review your cash inflows and outflows. Having children likely means more expenses and possibly less income due to maternity leave or a reduced workweek.
4. Stay out of lifestyle debt. Cash flow might be tight, and those baby clothes are oh, so cute, but avoid the temptation to use your credit card or line of credit for discretionary purchases or unnecessary splurges.
5. Set up a monthly saving plan for your children's education and take advantage of the available government grants. We prefer RESPs to Group Savings Plans. An easy way to start is to use the Universal Child Care credit of $100 per month you receive from the government for children under the age of six.
6. Don't neglect your financial future. Set up monthly savings for your goals—home ownership, retirement, etc. Even if it's a very small amount, it will help energize you and keep your attention on what's important to you.
7. Make sure you're taking advantage of all child care deductions and tax credits. For example, you can claim for daycare, nannies, summer camp, before- and after-school programs.

The child fitness and art tax credits each allow a tax credit up to $500 per child for qualifying programs. Statistics show that many Canadians don't take advantage of these programs. Do a little homework to find out what you might be missing out on.

8. Talk to your kids about money early—and often. Many of us say we never learned about money when we were young, so this is your chance to break the cycle. Consider giving your children an allowance so they can start to learn about money. Keep the messages positive and help them make good choices on how they spend their money.

Teens and Money

Many of our clients find they can rein in their own expenses but when it comes to their kids, they turn into 'marshmallow parents.' And so it was a real test for Frank and Allison when their 17-year-old daughter Vanessa wanted to go on a school trip. Not your average day trip, this was a 12-day expedition that was going to give Vanessa an opportunity to live in another culture, learn a language and volunteer to help kids in another country.

All laudable goals. And all adding up to $3,000. It was money that just hadn't been figured into this family's budget so this was a dilemma. The solution we came up with? A combination of student summer earnings, a small parental contribution and an IOU from Vanessa to her parents for a loan to be paid off from a part-time job.

"If we think she is ready to make sacrifices to go on this trip, we'd be inclined to do the same," Allison said. "However if it's just that she'll go if we do all the heavy financial lifting, maybe not."

The teen traveller was ready to make the sacrifices, the trip went off without a hitch, and any worries that Frank and Allison had about being too Scrooge-like with their daughter disappeared when an older sibling weighed in.

"Our son told us that he might be more fiscally responsible today if we had pushed such responsibilities onto him instead of letting him duck them," Frank later told us.

SO IF YOU'RE beginning to think your teen regards your wallet as a cash machine, it's time to change that expectation immediately.

8 TIPS TO TEACH YOUR TEENS ABOUT GOOD MONEY MANAGEMENT

1. **Give them an allowance.** It's okay if they make mistakes in their spending decisions; it's how they learn.

2. **Give them financial responsibilities.** What expenses are they expected to cover with their allowance? Bus fare, lunch money, clothes, cell phone, movies, slurpees?

3. **Talk to them about money.** You can't learn anything new if you never talk about it.

4. **Involve them in some of the decisions about family finances.** Give them a choice or hold a family vote. Should we buy a new TV or go on holiday? Do you want to play hockey at $600 a year or take weekly guitar lessons?

5. **Encourage them to save for things they really want or insist they pay half.** A trip with the school, a must-have pair of $200 jeans, spending money for your family holiday.

6. **Don't get your teens hooked on credit.** That means not continually shelling out money in return for half-hearted promises to pay it back.

7. **Don't let them off the hook.** If you do agree to advance them money, clearly set out the terms and stick to them. And don't bail them out if they spend all their money in the first

few days of getting their allowance. They need to learn to make it last.

8. **It's okay to say no.** They will thank you for it later (okay, much later, but they will thank you one day).

Aging Parents and Money

Karin wasn't sure when it happened, but sometime a few years ago she realized that tables were turning in her relationship with her parents. Although still extremely healthy and vibrant 70-year-olds, Karin's parents were starting to ask her for advice and she could feel a subtle shift in the power balance. She didn't (and still doesn't) feel ready for what's likely to come—but who ever is?

MOST OF THE children of aging parents we know are busy, stressed and ill-equipped to deal with the added time and financial demands of caring for elderly parents. And often the need to step in comes during a crisis. Needless to say, this isn't a great time to make the emotional, financial and legal decisions that are often necessary.

If at all possible, have a conversation with your parents early. Find out what your parents have in mind for their future, get a sense of where they stand financially and get an idea of the role that you and your siblings might be called upon to play. None of these points is easy to talk about and you must be sensitive and respect your parents' need for privacy, dignity and sense of control.

Here are some simple guidelines to help in developing a Caregiving Plan of Action:

1. Start your dialogue with parents and siblings as soon as possible—strive for practicality and openness. Remind yourself, and each other, that these issues will eventually have to be faced and that it is best to be prepared well in advance.

2. One of the chief objectives of your plan should be to maintain your parents' self-esteem and a degree of personal independence. Studies have shown most seniors want to stay in their own homes as long as possible.

3. Get informed. Find out what services and assistance are available in your community. Local seniors' centres can provide a wealth of information and advice.

4. Get a sense of your parents' financial capacity and their desires. Do they have enough money to cover medical expenses, the costs of home care or a retirement home? Do they have a retirement community in mind? Would they like to live nearer to you or other family? Or do they want to stay in their home as long as possible?

5. Find out where your parents keep financial and legal documents. You don't need to know all the details unless there's a crisis, but you do need to know how to access the information quickly and easily if something does happen.

6. Find out if your parents have up-to-date Wills, Powers of Attorney and health care directives. Gently encourage them to have their legal professional review and update these as needed.

7. Create a list of names and contact information for your parents' key professionals, such as doctors, lawyers, accountants, brokers, financial planners, bankers.

Don't be discouraged if you try to broach the topic with your parents and it's a non-starter. Be patient and gently persistent. (It took a couple of glasses of red wine to get the conversation going with Karin's father!)

Knowing where your parents stand on these issues and having a plan in place will save your family much grief later.

Next Steps

Through your reflections on the role of money in your life over the last few chapters, you may realize that there are areas that you need some help with—your relationship with money, challenging family dynamics or the more technical aspects of money like investing, retirement planning or cash flow management.

In the next chapter we'll look at a variety of professionals who can help you navigate your way to financial ease.

⟩ 5 ⟨

||||||||||||||||||||||||

HELP,
I NEED SOMEBODY!

Don't follow any advice, no matter how good,
until you feel as deeply in your spirit
as you think in your mind that the counsel is wise.

JOAN RIVERS

BEFORE DAN BECAME a money coaching client, he was shopping for a new investment advisor. He interviewed several to see if he could find a good fit. While he found all of the advisors he spoke with to be approachable and very knowledgeable, none of them could guarantee they would be able to predict the next market downturn in time to protect his investments from a drop in value. He was also a little disconcerted that one advisor's prediction about the market was the exact opposite of another's prediction. Disheartened, he came to this conclusion—"basically they have no idea."

While this statement may be a little jarring, we think Dan accurately captures how many people are feeling these days. If advisors don't know the answers, what are we paying them for and where does that leave us? As a consequence of the breakdown of trust in our so-called experts, there's been a big movement to the do-it-yourself model. This works well for some, but it leaves many people who are already stretched with life's responsibilities feeling even more stressed, vulnerable and unable to move forward with their finances.

Because of the increasing complexity of the financial landscape, high debt levels and the stomach-turning market conditions, we generally do recommend that you seek advice and delegate some of the responsibility for planning and managing your money. However, it's crucial that you have realistic expectations of what advisors can and cannot do and that you're the one who remains in charge of your money.

Financial Advice—A New Paradigm

Fortunately, there is a new advice model evolving in the marketplace. The old 'expert-client' model where the advisor supposedly knew all and the client was expected to know nothing is being replaced by a more collaborative relationship. Let's face it: financial advisors are neither soothsayers nor all-knowing experts. And thanks to the Internet, clients are much better informed than ever before.

This profound paradigm shift can be troubling for both the advisor and the client who aren't prepared for this change. However, when advisors are focused on helping clients become more educated and empowered with their money and clients take a more proactive role in their financial life, it can lead to a much healthier and mutually beneficial relationship.

Financial advisors can still be a valuable resource—you simply need to get more involved, redefine your expectations and learn how to work effectively with them.

Become an informed consumer of financial services

By becoming educated, involved and on top of your money, you will be in a better position to work more collaboratively with your financial advisors and to feel more confident and in control. You'll be an active partner in your financial affairs rather than a passive observer or helpless victim. (We cover the basics of investing in Chapter 10.)

Finding the Right Financial Advisor

So, how do you choose a financial advisor under this new paradigm? It starts with you being clear about your goals, the type of advice you're seeking, and what you expect of your advisor.

There is certainly no shortage of people willing to help you out with your money—the challenge is to find a qualified advisor who fits your unique needs, values, and financial situation.

The best way to get financial advice is to be very clear on what your challenges are and what problems you are looking for someone to help you solve.

Start your search by figuring out what type of advice you're looking for and how you want to pay for it. Ask yourself these questions:

1. **What do I need help with now?** Is it investing, planning and saving for the future, day-to-day cash management, getting out of debt, financial decisions relating to retirement or other life transitions?

2. **How do I want to pay for this advice?** Do I want to pay directly by writing a cheque for the advice or indirectly through product sales like investments, insurance, banking or credit counseling services?

   The terminology in the financial advice industry is not standardized, so be sure to ask questions and to clarify what you can expect from your advisor no matter what model of financial advice works best for you.

If you're looking for help with cash flow or debt management

The financial planning advice industry has largely focused on clients who have money to invest. But where do you turn if you need guidance and advice on how to better manage your day-to-day finances, start saving for your goals or get out of debt?

Money Coaches

If you're a well-paid professional juggling money, work and family, frustrated that you're not getting ahead financially due to debt or inadequate money management skills, then a 'fee for service' Money Coach may be the ticket. A Money Coach will help you clarify your goals, identify blocks to financial success and create a system to help you get out of debt and start allocating monies appropriately to your short, medium and long-term goals.

A key component to money coaching is to help clients shed negative attitudes and bad habits around money and to provide the structure, accountability and motivation to stop sabotaging their financial goals. Fees for a money coaching engagement typically range from $2,000 to $3,500.

At Money Coaches Canada, our Money Coaches do not sell investments or financial products and provide unbiased planning, education and advice. Not all Money Coaches work on a 'fee for service' basis, so be sure to ask.

Where to turn if you are too deep in debt

If you are struggling with debt, your options for advice will largely depend on the severity of your debt problem and your ability to repay your non-mortgage-related debt within a four to five year time period. While there is no shortage of alternatives, the quality and the ethics of the advice vary dramatically, so be very sure you find a service that meets your needs and you understand exactly what you are signing up for.

If your debt level (not including mortgage) is very high relative to your income and no matter how you crunch the numbers, the situation feels hopeless, then your best bet is to speak with a bankruptcy trustee about the options available to you. Fees and obligations vary depending on whether you decide to go the route of a bankruptcy or a consumer proposal.

There are other credit counseling or debt settlement consultants but many are not regulated so be sure that you are clear on what service they can provide to you and how you are actually paying for their services.

If you're looking for Long-term and Life Transitions Planning
If you're looking for recommendations on a broader range of financial concerns, including your life goals, cash flow, debt, investments, retirement, insurance and estate needs, a certified financial planner (CFP®) is your best bet. Financial planners generally fall into two categories:

1. **Financial Planners licensed to sell investments or insurance**
   Typically this type of financial planner will provide you with a financial plan for free if you purchase or plan to purchase investments or insurance with them (although a minimum investment may be required or implied). Others referred to as 'asset-based' financial planners may charge a fee for the plan then give you the option to invest or buy insurance from them.

2. **Financial Planners who don't sell financial products**
   'Fee for service' financial planners or Money Coaches charge clients a fee either hourly or by project. Fees for comprehensive financial planning typically range between $2,500 and $5,000 depending on the complexity of your planning needs. Note that some financial planners call themselves 'fee for service' but have affiliates in their company who are able to sell investments or financial products. Ask for clarification if you aren't sure.

Are you looking for investment advice or are you a do-it-yourself investor?
If you have investments, the first step is deciding if you want advice or if you want to handle your own investing. Whatever you decide, make it a conscious and considered choice.

The Do-It-Yourself Approach

Some people feel like they are the best captain of their ship and in this information age, you have unlimited access to information about specific funds, specific companies, market trends and more.

But do you have time or the expertise? You might save yourself a few dollars in fees, but if you're going to commit to managing your own investment portfolio, you have to be sure you have what it takes to do this successfully. Also, make sure you understand what fees even do-it-yourself investors have to pay and what service accompanies those fees.

Most banks and credit unions have discount brokerage departments that work well for do-it-yourself investors. You pay a smaller commission on buying and selling stocks and bonds than you would if you worked with an investment advisor who provides advice and helps select investments for you. You can open an investment account and buy mutual funds, individual stocks, bonds or cash investments. You can manage your own registered accounts like RSPS, RIFS and TFSAS.

There are also websites like globeinvestor.com that help you inventory and track your investments. These sites are free and may give you more detailed information than your investment statement.

So, managing your own investments will take time and you are still going to pay some fees. When you look at that, you may decide that the added cost associated with an advisor is worth the money. It's all a question of whether you are getting service and value.

Often the lowest cost option is going to give you the lowest amount of service. That can work very well if you want to do the groundwork involved in choosing, monitoring and maintaining your investment portfolio. In spite of the bad rap a lot of investment advisors are getting these days, finding an informed, trustworthy advisor just might save you a lot of time, headaches and confusion.

Working with an Investment Advisor

Investment advisors are typically compensated through commissions or charge a percentage of your investments usually in the 1% to 2% range, depending on the size of your portfolio. If you want investment advice by someone who is not managing your investments, that's harder to find.

Because of the securities legislation in Canada, only an advisor who is licensed through a qualified financial institution or portfolio management company is legally allowed to provide you with specific stock, bond or mutual fund recommendations. You can, however, pay an independent non-licensed advisor like a Money Coach for investment strategy advice, coaching or education—they just can't tell you what specific securities you should invest in.

Who Can Help You? How Can They Help?
And How Do They Get Paid?

If you don't want to manage your own investments, there are a lot of different advisors to choose from. To pick the right advisor, you have to match your needs to the advisor's services, and make sure you'll be able to work well together.

It used to be that choosing where to invest was simple. If you wanted a bank account or GIC you went to a bank. If you wanted stocks and bonds, you went to a stockbroker. Times have changed. You now have almost unlimited options, which is good, but it can take a bit of investigative work on your part.

To start, be clear on the amount you have to invest and your risk tolerance. That information will help to narrow the field of advisors that may be a good fit for you.

Your next step is to start asking friends and colleagues for referrals. But remember, they might have very different investment objectives, or they might require services that you do not. To be sure that you are getting a referral to the kind of advisor you want, it's important to understand what type of advisors are out there, what they can do for you and how they get paid.

Bank Branches

Banks are a good place to start if you haven't invested before and have less than $50,000. (You also have the option of online banks.)

Banks now have licensed mutual fund representatives in their branches who can help you invest in mutual funds, GICs and Canada Savings Bonds, either within your RSP or outside your RSP. You can usually open a discount brokerage account through your local branch as well. Most branch staff are paid a salary and many of them are paid a bonus based on a variety of sales criteria.

Mutual Fund Companies

Some mutual fund companies have in-house advisors that provide investment planning and advice. These advisors only sell their company's funds. A few examples are Leith Wheeler Investment Counsel, Steadyhand Investment Funds, Phillips, Hager and North Investment Management Services, and Mawer Investment Management.

Financial Planners

Commission or 'asset-based' financial planners provide investment management services and typically are paid commissions or a percentage of assets if they manage your investments. When a fee is based on a percentage of your investments, usually it's in the 1% to 2% range, depending on the size of your portfolio. Most financial planners licensed to sell investments can choose from a wide variety of mutual fund companies, and some can manage individual stocks and bonds as well.

Brokers or Investment Advisors

It used to be that most stockbrokerage companies were owned privately. Now all the major banks have in-house brokerage operations and there are relatively few independent brokerage companies. Generally brokers, or investment advisors as they are more commonly called today, work with clients who have at least $100,000 to $200,000. If they've been in the business for a while, this might be as high as $500,000 or more.

They research, advise and process investment trades on your behalf. Some investment advisors also provide financial planning services. You can buy virtually any investment or financial product through an investment advisor, including mutual funds, and they are compensated either by commission whenever they buy or sell investments for you or, if it is a 'asset-based' account, the fee is a percentage of the investments they manage for you. Commissions depend on the price and quantity of the investments you are buying and selling, but it is typical to pay $200 or more per trade. Fees for 'asset-based' accounts are generally between 1% and 2% of the value of the investments that they hold on your behalf.

For instance, if you have $150,000 invested with an investor advisor and their fee is 2%, you would pay $3,000 per year.

Investment Counsellors or Private Investment Managers

Investment counsellors, or private investment managers, deal with clients who have at least $500,000 and sometimes more. They offer highly specialized and personalized investment management services to their clients and they typically charge 1% to 1.5% of the value of the investments that they manage on your behalf.

IT IS IMPORTANT to keep in mind that there are also some advisors who work in very specialized fields. Some work in specialized areas of the market, such as mining stocks or ethical investments, some have minimum investment criteria for new clients, and others specialize in working with clients in particular industries. So if you ask a friend for a referral, also ask why they chose their advisor.

Questions to Ask Potential Financial Advisors

Once you have decided what type of financial advice is best suited to your needs, the next step is to find an advisor who has the right experience and credentials. Look also for someone that you trust to be open, respectful and non-judgmental. Here are some questions to ask:

- Can you describe the type of clients you serve?
- What are your qualifications?
- Do you have a minimum investment or net worth requirement?
- What are the fees for your services and any products/ investments you sell?
- How are you compensated?
- What products and services do you offer?
- How often will we meet and how much contact will we have?
- Will I be working with you or with your assistant?

Additional questions for advisors who manage investments:
- What is your investment philosophy or approach?
- What can I expect from you in market downturns?
- How will I know how much money I'm making?
- How is my rate of return reported to me?
- How often will I receive my statements? Will you explain them to me?

Even if you work with a financial advisor, it is up to you to educate yourself. It's about *delegating, not abdicating* responsibility for your money. If you are currently working with an advisor but don't know the answers to the questions above, then it's time to ask them.

If your advisor is used to you participating more passively in meetings, you might encounter resistance as you try to assert your financial authority. Some advisors see your questions as a threat or possibly as a hint that you're not happy and plan to move your money. Remind yourself that it's your money and you have a right to be involved and to ask all the questions you want.

And trust your gut—if you don't feel good about your connection with your advisor, then it may be time to move on to someone else.

▸ 6 ◂

||||||||||||||||||||||||

GETTING WHAT
YOU REALLY WANT

The world stands aside to let anyone
pass who knows where he [she] is going.
DAVID STARR JORDAN

IF YOU'RE SERIOUS about taking charge of your finances and using money as a tool to support your life, then you need to create a plan for your finances that starts with you and what you want. While you've probably heard that it's a good idea to have a financial plan, you might be thinking, "Sure, I'll make a plan when I have money to plan." But it really works the other way around.

Having a plan that helps you articulate your goals and define your financial starting point sends a strong message that you are serious about attracting and managing the money you need to create the life you want.

A financial plan is a roadmap to help you define your financial life goals and to give you the tools, information and structure to organize your finances to live the life you want.

· How do I balance today's goals with a secure financial future?
· Do I have enough money to retire comfortably?

- Which investments or financial products are suited to my needs?
- What do I need to know to make the best financial decisions?

A financial plan will help you answer these questions in an organized, structured manner. By creating a financial plan, you will know what steps you need to take to get from where you are now to where you want to be.

It needs to start with who *you* are, what *you* want out of your life and with *your* unique dreams and goals. You can't create a solid plan for your finances without having it deeply rooted in your plan for your life. Otherwise you don't stand much of a chance of being motivated or staying committed to your financial plan. Financial drift, avoidance and over-spending are often the result of a lack of clarity about your life priorities. If there is no reason not to spend, guess what, we spend! The clearer you are about the life you want to create, the less likely you'll be distracted by bright shiny objects and other distractions that come with the messages that bombard us daily.

The Power Behind the Plan

Dreams and goals have power. When you dream, you think creatively about the life you would like to live. When you set goals, you tell yourself and those around you that you are working towards something that is important to you. When you set goals to attain your dream life, you are saying "I've finished waiting—I'm going to make this happen."

There are a lot of people pulling at your pocket and countless pressures on your life, but when you are clear about the life you want, you are free to set your own agenda for your finances and your life.

You might be thinking that being 'good with money' is about being clever with numbers. And while financially secure people do keep a close eye on their bottom line, the biggest secret to their success is that they know what they consider to be a good life and they do what they need to do to live it.

It's not a coincidence that people who focus on living happy, fulfilling lives often end up making more *and saving more* money.

Your goals and aspirations are the greatest motivators you have to attain and maintain financial control. When you're tempted by old habits, it's going to be the things you really want that motivate you to stay in control.

A Plan Begins With a Dream

In our culture, people think 'dreamer' is a bad word. What's worse, people seem to enjoy using money as the prime excuse to throw cold water on their dreams. The way you use your money can stop you from living the life you want, or it can empower you to live the life you want. The choice is up to you.

So the very first step in your financial plan is to have a strong vision of what you want before you get into the numbers. This is your place to dream and think about what you're truly passionate about. Often until we take the time to sit down and really think about what we want, we don't identify our goals and dreams. And if you don't know what you want, it's pretty hard to get it.

At this stage in the planning process don't worry too much about practicality or reality. It's easy to hold back and not give yourself permission to dream. Instead start by thinking about what you would do with your life if money was no object. Don't censor yourself, just write down the things that come to you. They can just be ideas or intentions at this stage. You may even be surprised by how few of your goals actually involve money.

IF MONEY WASN'T AN ISSUE,
WHAT WOULD YOU DO?

This page is for your dreams. Don't filter. Don't hold back. Nothing is silly. Just write. You'll "get real" on other pages. Everything is permitted here. Surprise yourself. Keep going. Even if you are in debt, even if you don't think you can afford it, even if every other moment of the day you are 'practical,' write down what matters most here.

What future do you see?

_____

Where would you live?

_____

Where would you work?

_____

How much would you work?

_____

What would you be doing?

_____

Who would you be doing it with?

_____

What brings you joy?

_____

What contributions would you make?

_____

What legacy would you leave?

_____

Aligning Your Money with Your Goals

Anna and Joel dreamt of owning their own home. They were paying a fortune to live in a small basement apartment. They had debt, and they were in the habit of getting out of town on the weekends to enjoy a better quality of life. Because she couldn't believe they would ever buy a home, Anna would buy $100 Home Lottery tickets in the hopes of getting lucky.

They wanted a house, but they didn't let themselves want it enough to make it a priority. Instead they squandered money and perpetuated a spending pattern that made home ownership seem impossible.

Anna and Joel went through our money coaching program. They saw a house, and the stability that it would provide as a key part of their dream life. As a goal, they wrote down that they wanted to buy a house in a year. Then we helped them figure out what it would take to achieve the goal.

The couple stopped spending money on trips and takeout. With their new consciousness about their spending, they were able to cut costs, pay off their debt and have enough money for a down payment in only eight months.

That is the power of aligning your money with your goals. Once Anna and Joel allowed themselves to believe they could own a home, they put all their resources towards making the goal a reality.

MOST OF US have more power than we think—sometimes all it takes is more clarity and a belief that we deserve to have our heart's desire.

Once you have a clear vision of what you want and where you want to go, the next step is to start breaking down your vision and your intentions into more concrete goals.

Our goals are the carrot, the motivator, the reason we work hard or work smarter. A strong goal gives you a reason to make difficult choices, to be more careful with your money, and to spend less and earn more.

People who have a clear goal find it easier to do what it takes. They're motivated and spurred on by what they can see ahead. They have good reasons to make changes. Everyone's dreams and goals are different. Figuring out what will spur you on is the key. For some it's starting a family, buying a house, getting married, taking time to travel, early retirement, or a desire for financial independence. What are your motivating goals?

Measurable, Achievable and True

The plain and simple truth about goals is that they have to be measurable, achievable, and heartfelt or you might as well throw your pennies in a wishing well. It's all too easy to take on society's goals or other people's goals, but that makes it hard—if not impossible—to feel truly energized and committed to them.

Goals should be:

Measurable so that you know when you've achieved them.

Achievable so that both your desire and the ability to achieve your goals will motivate you to keep working towards them.

True to your heart so that you are willing to stretch yourself and imagine your way past hurdles. If you aren't willing to do what it takes, you have to ask yourself if the goal is true to you.

Time and Money

Dreams are pretty abstract. Goals break dreams into bite-sized pieces. You identify an action that you can take, attach it to a time line, and figure out how much money, if any, you will need to make it happen.

Here's an example of how one woman turned her vision of the future into a series of goals.

JESSIE IS A SINGLE MOM with an average-paying job and $80,000 owing on her townhouse. Ultimately, Jessie wants a master's degree, a close-knit family, a job she loves, adventures with her kids, and to not have to worry about being able to support herself or her family.

That's the dream. These are the goals she set for herself:

GOAL	COST/VALUE	TIME FRAME
1. Start a 2-year part-time online degree	$10,000	In 8 months
2. Sell my home in Vancouver	Ask $425,000	In 6 months
3. Buy a home near my sister in Victoria	Max $410,000	In 8 months
4. Take a leave of absence to spend time with kids and find a rewarding new job	$12,000	In 18 months
5. Buy kayaks for the family	$5,000	In 2 years
6. Set up RSPs for me and RESPs for the kids	$2,000−$4,000	Contribute every year

She's halfway there. She knows what she wants, when she wants it, and how much she needs.

Now that Jessie is clear on her goals she can choose how to go about achieving them.

Earn a little extra now before going back to school? Save a little extra by riding her bike to work for a year? Get the kids to do the dusting instead of the cleaning lady?

Goal-Setting Hints

Review your dreams

You wrote down your dreams so that you could visualize your best life. Now write down your goals on the next page so that you can start living it. You are identifying priorities for your money and your time, so make sure you set goals that will get you what you really want.

Become debt-free

You probably didn't write 'debt-free' on your dream page, but it was implied by all the wonderful things you could be doing with your money if it wasn't servicing your debts. If you make being debt-free a goal, you are that much closer to achieving every other goal on your page.

Put yourself on the same page with your family

If you are in a relationship or if you have dependents, your goals, like your finances, will be impacted by the significant people in your life. You need to stand up for what you believe is important for you and your family, but everyone needs to work together. If you are single with no dependents, you may have it easier because the only person you really have to please is yourself.

It Starts Here

Building a financial plan is about planning to achieve your goals. So what are yours? *(see worksheet on facing page)*

Commitment

The C-word is a big one. Some people resist setting goals because they think, "Something might happen. I might change my mind. What if I get hit by a bus? What if I change jobs? What if I come into money? I just want to take life as it comes."

YOUR LIFE AND FINANCIAL GOALS

What do you need to do to live your dream life?

GOAL	COST/VALUE	TIME FRAME
1. e.g. Travel—Europe	$10,000	In 1 year
2.		
3.		
4.		
5.		
6.		
7.		
8.		
9.		

Goals are dreams with a deadline.
Dreams without a deadline are just wishes.

Being easygoing, and free to roll with the surprises life throws at you, is a very valuable attribute. But "rolling" with change suggests you had a specified course, something has come up, and now you are going to make adjustments. You are still committed to living your best life, you are just open to the possibility that there are new ways of achieving it.

Having a plan based on your goals means you have a framework. That framework will actually make it easier for you to 'roll' with change. It is a support system; it doesn't lock you into a pigeonhole. And the best thing about learning how to align a financial plan with your goals is that if your goals change in the future, you'll know how to change your plan accordingly.

A very real reason that people don't commit to their goals and to a plan is that ultimately they're afraid to change their behaviour. That doesn't have to be your story. You are here to adjust your thinking, your habits and your financial behaviour to suit your best life.

Tell people that you are committed to your goals. Give them the opportunity to support your efforts. People are inspired by those with conviction—and in the process of inspiring others, you will inspire yourself.

Be proactive. Stave off temptation by being honest with people about your commitment to your goals. Let them know that your life is good and that your finances are spoken for. When people understand that you are making positive changes, they often want to help. If some people respond negatively to your efforts, it's just because they can't see what you see. If they can't support your goals, move on.

Be positive. If you hear yourself say "I can't" too many times, you start to believe it. The whole point of gaining financial control is so that you *can* choose to do what you want with your money and your life. The benefit of having a plan is that it will make it easier to choose to spend your money on things that support your life. And easier to choose *not* to spend your money on things that don't.

So if someone or something tempts you, instead of saying "I can't," which suggests you are denying yourself, try saying "I'm saving for a …" It will make a world of difference to your mindset and to your finances.

Creative Ways to Think About Balancing Conflicting Goals

In the goal-setting exercise, you might have found that there are conflicting goals or there doesn't seem to be enough money to go around for all your goals. It can be a balancing act and trade-offs are often necessary—at least temporarily. Some goals might need to be set aside for a time, others can be dropped or readjusted. By committing to your goals in writing you are setting strong intentions for your future, which can help you clarify which goals have staying power.

Common examples of conflicting goals

Don't worry if you have conflicting goals, everybody has them at some point.

PAY DOWN DEBT **AND** SAVE FOR RETIREMENT:
Angie and Todd are absolutely committed to paying down their debt. That is their number one goal. But they are also committed to saving for retirement.

When they looked at their cash flow, it seemed they weren't earning enough to cover their basic expenses, service their loan, and contribute to an RSP on a monthly basis. Some months when they tried to do everything, they would just end up having to dip into their line of credit—and that was going against their number one goal.

So they came up with this creative solution. On a monthly basis, they pay their expenses in full and they pay down their loan. They aren't overspending, so they aren't sliding further into debt. And every month they can watch the debt decrease, which is great motivation to carry on.

At tax time, between the two of them, they'll get a $5,000 income tax refund. They'll use the refund to contribute to RSPs. That not only satisfies their second goal of saving for their future, but it's a strategy they can repeat year after year.

PAY OFF THE MORTGAGE **AND** SAVE FOR A HOLIDAY:

Tom is really close to paying off his mortgage. Every month, he pays an extra $300 on it. If he keeps up these payments, he'll own his own home within five years. That is a huge achievement and a meaningful goal.

But he also really wants to take a holiday this summer—the timing isn't great financially. It is his sister's 50th birthday and everyone is planning a two-week vacation in Spain.

Tom knows he only has enough money to meet one of these competing goals this year, but instead of giving up on either, he uses his creativity and motivation to do both.

Sticking to his goal of paying off the mortgage within five years is important, but it would mean so much to get the whole family together this year. So he decides to keep up the extra monthly mortgage payments, and he uses his visions of azure beaches to push himself to earn a little extra money for the holiday.

He'll use his enthusiasm to hold garage sales, pick up overtime, and take on small contracts that he can do on weekends. And when he finds the extra work tiring, he'll remind himself it isn't forever—it's for Spain!

START A BUSINESS **AND** SAVE FOR THE FUTURE:

Joss plans to open her massage therapy clinic this summer. Starting her own business is a dream come true, but it certainly puts a lot of pressure on her cash flow.

In order to feel secure in her new business, she really wants to know that she has money set aside for emergencies and retirement. So contributing to her savings on a monthly basis is a goal she is committed to.

Being the savvy entrepreneur that she is, Joss decided to look for ways to cover some of her expenses with something other than money.

Since she can't trade services for GICs, she'll use her earnings for her savings, and she'll trade services for things like setting up her website, bookkeeping and business coaching. It isn't hard to find service providers who need massage therapy, and it's great for her to work with well-connected business people who might be able to refer business to her in the future.

PAY OFF STUDENT LOANS **AND** SAVE FOR MATERNITY LEAVE:
Kim and Brad have about $9,000 left on their student loans. They are both earning money now, but the weight of the debt has put a lot of pressure on the young couple for a number of years.

They would like to pay off the loans this year, but now that Kim is pregnant, they also both want to take six months off work, one after the other. The baby's first year is too precious to miss. This time-sensitive goal really made them take a hard look at their options.

Believe it or not, they have committed to reducing their expenses and paying off the $9,000 loan before the baby is born. That means paying $1,500 per month towards the loans for the next six months. That's $1,000 more than they had previously paid each month.

This is a great plan for balancing potentially conflicting goals for two reasons:

By getting rid of the debt, they're removing a serious source of pressure on the family.

By cutting back their monthly living expenses for the six months before the baby is born, they'll be prepared to live off a reduced income while they both enjoy time off with their newborn.

The two are both really motivated. They've gone down to one car, they're cutting back on takeout dinners, books, clothes and all the extras that aren't nearly as important to them as starting this new phase of their life debt-free.

If you seem to have conflicting goals you might want to:
- Use your tax refund, birthday money, bonuses or other windfalls to pay for one goal, and use your monthly income to pay for the other.
- Earn more, and use your goals to motivate you to find ways to do that.
- Use something other than money to achieve a goal, or part of a goal.
- Cut your expenses enough that you can save for both goals. Again, you'll need to believe in the goals for motivation.
- Be patient. Don't pressure yourself (or your spouse) to achieve all your goals at once. Your plan should ease your burden, not add to it.

If you have an immediate or time-sensitive goal, you might simply decide to focus all your resources there.

For example, once you are pregnant, a maternity leave isn't something you can put off. Having a nest egg may do more than support you financially; it might actually help to bring down your stress levels as a new parent. So temporarily, you might choose to make building up your savings a priority. If you decide to temporarily put a goal on hold, set a date to start supporting that goal again. Keep a date and cost attached to your goals—even if the date is four years from now.

Stay flexible and adapt: That's the key to using your goals as motivators for financial control. If you feel like you're in conflict, you'll feel pressure. And that can impair your ability to see your options.

Review and Revise
You aren't carving your goals, or your financial plan, in stone. You can try them out. See how they feel. Think about them. Talk about them. If something isn't sitting right, make adjustments.

You should pull out your plan at least once a year to check in with yourself. Acknowledge and reward your achievements. Look back at where you were when you started—but for now, just get started.

As you build your financial plan over the next few chapters, you will make decisions about how much to spend, save, invest, and borrow. Ultimately, the best financial strategies will depend on going back to your goals and making decisions that will support the vision of the life you want to create for yourself and your family.

KNOWLEDGE
SYSTEMS
TOOLS

▸ 7 ◂

||||||||||||||||||||||||||

YOUR FINANCIAL
STARTING POINT

I'm living so far beyond my income
that we may almost be said to be living apart.
E.E. CUMMINGS

SPENDING MONEY isn't bad. Debt isn't even necessarily bad. But as anyone who has ever seen a single-digit bank account knows, no money and no plan means no choices.

Give Yourself the Freedom to Choose
To gain and maintain financial control you need to understand how your money comes in and how it goes out. It is about awareness. And with awareness comes freedom.

This chapter will help you build your awareness about your current financial situation. It is also an opportunity to reflect on whether or not your spending is in line with your values. By the end, you will know your current net worth, your current spending patterns and you will have a *Spending and Savings Plan* that will help you to make financial decisions that work for you.

Knowing where you stand will give you a good sense of where you are today and help you start to figure out what you need to do to get where you want to go, and ideally reach the goals you set in the previous chapter.

Net Worth

Your net worth is the key number to know when starting your plan as it will be the benchmark for you to see if you are making progress.

Net worth is a financial snapshot of where you stand at one point in time. It is the difference between what you OWN and what you OWE.

Assets (what you own) – Liabilities (what you owe) = Net Worth

- Common examples of Assets: house, car, cash, antique collection, RSPs and pension savings
- Common examples of Liabilities: student loan, credit card debt, mortgage, line of credit

Your net worth can be improved by decreasing debt, committing more money to your investments, earning a greater rate of return on your investments, or enjoying an increase in the value of your assets. For example, an increase in the value of your home will improve your net worth.

We recommend you review your net worth at least once a year to see the progress or lack thereof. We find that many people are pleasantly surprised at how much their net worth has grown from one year to the next. Contributing even small amounts to your RSP each year and paying your mortgage or debts can make a big difference. And it's nice to take stock and see how well you've done each year. If your net worth isn't growing over the year it might highlight some problem areas you need to work on in the coming year.

Uses of Net Worth

- To understand your current financial picture
- To track your progress year to year—it is a quick indication of forward and backward motion

- To apply for a bank loan or mortgage—lenders need to see your whole financial picture
- To draw up your Will and for estate planning

Instructions for Completing a Net Worth Statement

Start by filling in the details of your current financial picture.

In the *Details For Your Net Worth Statement* worksheet on the next page, write down all the things you own: house, car, RSPs, stocks, bonds, cash accounts, pensions, etc.

Include the financial institution your RSPs or savings are with, and any additional details, such as the year and model of your car, the current price of the stocks you own and their original price.

Then list your debts and the amounts owing: your mortgage, line of credit, student loans, credit cards, personal loans, family loans, outstanding bills and other items.

Make note of who the lender is; how much you are repaying per week, per month or per year; what the interest rate is and, for credit cards and lines of credit, what your credit limit is.

Use the boxes on the details page to total your assets and liabilities. Then carry the totals forward to the *Net Worth Statement* worksheet on the following page. Then, tally everything up to see your net worth.

The difference between your assets and your liabilities is your net worth. If you have more debt than you have assets you will have a negative net worth, and if you have more assets than debts then your net worth will be positive. Your net worth, whether it is positive or negative, is simply a starting point, it's neither good nor bad, it's just where you are today. But the goal is to see it grow over time.

DETAILS FOR YOUR NET WORTH STATEMENT

Current Date:

1. **CASH & DEPOSIT ACCOUNTS**   Amount $ _____
   Chequing   _____
   Savings   _____
   Other   _____
   Other   _____

2. **OUTSTANDING DEBT**   Financial Institution   Amount $ _____
   Credit Card #1   _____   _____
   Credit Card #2   _____   _____
   Loan   _____   _____
   Line of Credit   _____   _____
   Car Loan   _____   _____
   Home Buyer's Plan   _____   _____

3. **RSP's** $ _____

   Financial Institution   Amount
   _____   _____
   _____   _____
   _____   _____

4. **TAX FREE SAVINGS ACCOUNTS** $ _____

   Financial Institution   Amount
   _____   _____
   _____   _____

5. **NON - RSP INVESTMENTS** $ _____
   (eg. GICs, CSBs, Stocks, Employee Share Purchase Plan, Mutual Funds)

   Financial Institution   Amount
   _____   _____
   _____   _____
   _____   _____

6. **PRINCIPAL RESIDENCE**   *Current Value of Home:* $ _____
   Mortage Company   _____   *Mortgage Balance:* $ _____

7. **VEHICLE(S)**   Type   **Current Value** $ _____
   Vehicle #1   _____   _____
   Vehicle #2   _____   _____

8. **PENSION - DEFINED CONTRIBUTION**   *Current Value:* $ _____

9. **PENSION - DEFINED BENEFIT**
   Monthly benefit at age 65   _____

10. **REAL ESTATE - OTHER**   *Current Value of Property* $ _____
    Mortage Company   _____   *Mortgage Balance:* $ _____

11. **OTHER** $ _____

NET WORTH STATEMENT

Current Date:

	ASSETS	LIABILITIES

INVESTMENT ASSETS AND LIABILITIES

CASH & DEPOSIT ACCOUNTS

OUTSTANDING DEBT

RSPs

TFSAs

NON - RSP INVESTMENTS

OTHER: _____

OTHER: _____

Total Investment Assets and Liabilities: $ _____ $ _____

LONG-TERM ASSETS AND LIABILITIES

PRINCIPAL RESIDENCE

VEHICLE(S)

PENSION - DEFINED CONTRIBUTION

REAL ESTATE - OTHER

OTHER: _____

Total Long-Term Assets & Liabilities: $ _____ $ _____

TOTAL ASSETS AND LIABILITIES $ _____ $ _____

NET WORTH (Assets - Liabilities) $ _____

Your Spending and Savings Plan

Managing your cash flow is key to your financial success. How well you manage your money today can have a direct influence on how much money you have available for goals and your future.

To be successful with money it is imperative that you look at how money flows into your household (e.g., income, bonuses, tax refunds, or government benefits, etc.) and how it flows out (spending, saving, bills, charity, etc.).

This is often the most dreaded part of money management and it's one people often prefer to avoid.

THE REACTION from a client of ours at the mention of cash flow is typical:

"Oh gawd, I'm afraid you're going to talk about a budget."

Why, we asked, would she be afraid of that?

"I'm afraid you're going to tell me I can't do what I want to do," she answered.

We told her that if she's spending more money than she is bringing in, she'll run into problems. But she didn't want to acknowledge that, in fact, she just wanted to ignore that potential predicament.

CREATING A *Spending and Savings Plan* isn't about restrictions; it's about making conscious decisions. We know it can be scary to take a close look at your spending, but until you take that first step, you won't be able to improve your situation. And you'll continue to wake up in the middle of the night worrying about how you are going to meet the bills.

Sometimes our clients say, "Oh, I can't afford that." That may be true, but all too often the affordability comes down to personal choice. Maybe you can't afford a new computer. Or maybe that new computer just wasn't as important to you as buying $200 jeans instead of $50 ones, or getting those new $150 shoes in all three colours instead of settling for just one pair.

Perhaps you really can't save money for a down payment on a home. Or perhaps if you were driving a Toyota Echo instead of an SUV you'd have a few hundred dollars extra every month to bolster your home buying account.

We all have our financial foibles and we make choices, often without realizing they are choices. If you think about the spending and saving exercise, it's all about shedding light on how we live our financial lives and about making good choices rather than about the more negative connotations of control and restraint.

Successfully Managing your Spending and Savings is your Key to Financial Control.

Tracking your savings and spending (and being aware of your own personal patterns) will give you an awareness that has more long-term value than anything you can invest in, buy or sell.

The most important and most overlooked financial concept is this: SPEND LESS THAN YOU EARN.

Obvious, right? And yet, according to Statistics Canada, more than 50% of Canadians currently spend more than they earn.

If you understand clearly what money is coming in and what's going out, then you're in a position to make informed, conscious decisions about your money and your life. You can use your money to build the life you want instead of building debt and financial insecurity.

Doesn't sound like fun? Here's the fun part: Once you have allocated the money for the must-have categories, whether it's rent, the mortgage, groceries or other essentials, you can decide what else is important to you and add in those categories.

This is where you get to make choices and as easy as that sounds, it isn't. Many of our clients come to us because they have been unwilling or unsure of how to make those choices.

The *Spending and Savings Plan* worksheet will help you analyze your current income, as well as your spending and saving patterns, and identify expenses you can trim to free up more money for your goals.

If you are seeing that...
- you're spending more on your cell phone and Internet than you're putting towards RSPS
- your rent or mortgage and other shelter costs are more than half of your take-home pay
- the money you spend on eating out, coffees, lunches and takeout meals could finance a luxurious trip to Hawaii each year (or could feed a family of five!)

... then it all starts to make sense as to why you might not be getting ahead. Why you can't afford to take a vacation every year, why you are still adding to your debt and why you're stressed about money. Just seeing these numbers on paper—in black and white—can spur you on to make changes.

Where Does My Money Go?
We have clients who feel money is just trickling out of a hole in their pockets but they're not really sure where it's all going or why there's nothing left at the end of the month.

We had a client who was desperate to travel but she could never save enough for a $500 plane ticket. Helping her fill out her *Spending and Savings Plan* worksheet, she was shocked to discover she was spending $1,500 on lattes every year.

"I could go on holiday to Thailand," she said. While perhaps the cost of her Thailand vacation was underestimated, it did make her realize that the reason she couldn't travel wasn't due to some outside factor beyond her control—it was a choice she was making.

ANOTHER CLIENT loved finding the perfect gifts. And by perfect, we mean pricey.

"How much do you spend on gifts every month?" we asked.

She thought for a minute or two.

"Maybe $200 a month?" she answered.

Her credit cards told a different story. Christmas was an extravaganza—it was more like $200 and more per person on the gift list—and that didn't count birthdays, retirement presents, wedding gifts and other special occasion spending.

There was no easy way to break the truth to her. So we put the question to her so she could decide.

"Given your income and your goals, is this an appropriate amount of money to be spending on gifts?"

When she realized that it wasn't just a simple matter of whether or not she could afford that enormous gift budget, but a choice she could make—having enough money to meet her own goals or spending on gifts at a rate she thought people expected—the answer was clear to her. And it came as a relief. Instead of struggling to keep up with expectations, she started dealing with what she had and as a result the gift spending became more innovative and more meaningful. Gone was the guilt—"Is my present going to be as good as the next one at this wedding?" And with it the guilt of adding yet another item to her credit card bill.

YOUR SPENDING AND SAVINGS PLAN: *(worksheet on page 91)*
You'll need to collect a few things to get started.
Try not to worry about what you are going to find out. Just fill in the boxes. If it turns out that you spend more than you earn, see if you can find a way to reduce your expenses or think creatively about how to make more money.

Pull out the last three months of bank and credit card statements. These will give you an itemized list of your spending. (If you use cash, estimate your expenses. Then, keep your receipts for the next month and go back over your estimates to confirm.)

Review your statements. You want to look at all three months so that you can get an average of what you have been spending on clothes, food, gas, eating out, etc.

There are always irregularities. If you used the last three months of information to estimate your expenses, you may need to make adjustments if the months you've tracked are out of the ordinary. You will also need your recent paycheque stubs to find your *net income* (the amount you take home).

If you get paid every two weeks, we recommend you use the amount you take home over two paycheques as your monthly income. There will be two months a year when you receive an extra paycheque. Make a note of that—if you plan to live off of two paycheques a month, you'll be able to use those extra paydays to boost your savings or pay down debt.

If your employer deducts RSP contributions, charitable donations or anything over and above the usual tax deductions, make a note of that too. Those expenses don't need to be shown on your cash flow because you have already accounted for them by using your net income as a starting point.

If you are self-employed or work on commission, determining a monthly income can be a challenge. We suggest that you try paying yourself a 'regular salary' every month. What is a reasonable amount of money that you can count on? Use the minimum amount for planning purposes. This way you know you can live on the minimum and any extra can go towards building up a buffer for slow times, holidays or an investment in your business.

Now you can get started on filling in your Spending and Savings Plan.

Put down what you would normally spend in the first two columns of the *Spending and Savings Plan* (multiply by 12 to get the annual amount or divide the annual number by twelve to get the monthly amounts).

Start by filling out your regular monthly income and then do some easy things like regular monthly expenses (rent or mortgage payments)—this will get the momentum going.

Then plunk in some average expenses. What did the last three months of spending tell you? What was your average grocery bill for the month? Clothes? Gas?

But what about everything else? How much do you spend on parking, eating out, lunches, coffees? What if you have friends over for dinner or you go to their house and bring a bottle of wine or flowers?

Things like clothes and gifts might be harder to estimate accurately. But think about how often you go clothes shopping—how much do you spend each time you go?

For gifts, make a list of all the people you tend to buy gifts for as well as for which occasion. For example, you may buy your mother a birthday gift, a Christmas gift, a Mother's Day gift; you may even send something on your parents' anniversary or just because. How much do you spend on each gift?

Don't forget to include the cost of wrapping, a card and shipping if necessary. Go through this same exercise for all the people you buy gifts for. Then total up all the numbers. Don't forget other occasions that could call for presents, like weddings, baby showers, retirements, the end-of-year

teacher's present, or the collection for your children's soc-
cer coach. You might be surprised at how much you spend on
gifts for others. Most people really underestimate how much
they spend in this area. More often than not the total adds up
to double what they first estimated.

If you have children, go through a similar exercise for all
their sports and activities. These expenses can really add up,
and if a few of them come due at the same time, this can cause
stress on your cash flow. Tally up all the activities and related
costs that might be associated with activities your children
participate in such as sports, sports equipment, music lessons, summer camps, art classes, school fees and supplies,
and field trips.

Think about expenses that only come up a few times a
year, such as car repairs, vet bills, and travel. Estimate a total
for those expenses, divide the total by 12, and put that figure
in the monthly column. You may not pay these expenses in
12 monthly installments, but imagine you are setting money
aside each month so that you have the total amount when the
expense or bill comes due. (More about setting up a money
management system in Chapter 8.)

Interpreting the Numbers

Preparing a *Spending and Savings Plan* can be an eye-open-
ing experience. You might be surprised to see how well you
are already doing. Or you might see that you've left yourself
considerable room for improvement.

The first step is to add up the numbers in the income and
expenses sections. Then subtract what you are spending from
what you are earning to come up with your cash flow surplus
or deficit. You may be pleasantly surprised to see that there is
$500 left at the end of the month, or you may be disappointed
to find out you are spending $300 or $400 more than you are
bringing in.

SPENDING AND SAVINGS PLAN

NET INCOME	Monthly	Annual	Changes
Income - Me (after tax and deductions)			
Income - Spouse (after tax and deductions)			
Bonus/Overtime			
Government Benefits			
Rental Income			
Other			
TOTAL NET INCOME			

EXPENSES:

MAIN CHEQUING - Monthly Fixed Costs	Monthly	Annual	Changes
Rent / Mortgage			
Condo/Strata Fees			
Property Insurance (if paid monthly)			
Property Taxes (if paid monthly)			
Gas or Oil (for heating)			
Hydro			
Phone			
Cable			
Internet			
Cell Phone(s)			
House Alarm			
Childcare / Allowance / Children's Expenses			
Life Insurance Premiums			
Disability Insurance Premiums			
Health Premiums			
Vehicle Payments			
RSP			
RESPs			
Non-RSP Savings			
Bank Fees			
Vehicle Insurance (if paid monthly)			
Charitable Donation			
Clubs or Gym Membership (if paid monthly)			
Credit Card #1 Pymt			
Credit Card #2 Pymt			
Personal Loan / Student Loan Payment			
Line of Credit Payment			
Other			
Total Monthly Fixed Costs			

MONTHLY SPENDING - Chequing #2	Monthly	Annual	Changes
Groceries & Cleaning Supplies			
Pet Food and Treats			
Pharmacy, Toiletries			
Gas for Vehicle			
Taxis / Bus/ Parking			
Snacks and Lunches at work			
Entertainment - Dining out, Movies, etc.			
Alcohol - (beer/wine) and/or Cigarettes			
Other			
Total Monthly Spending			

SAVINGS ACCOUNTS - Lump Sum and Annual Expenses	Monthly	Annual	Changes
Fixed Annual & Lump Sum Expenses			
Property Taxes (if paid annually)			
Vehicle Insurance (if paid annually)			
Property Insurance (if paid annually)			
Clubs & Memberships (if paid annually)			
Magazine Subscriptions			
Costco Membership/Credit Card Annual Fees			
Professional / Accounting Fees			
Variable Annual & Lump Sum Expenses			
Home Repairs, Furniture and Household Items			
Vehicle Repairs and Maintenance			
Medical, Dental, Glasses, Contacts			
Personal Care (hair care, cosmetics, dry cleaning)			
Clothing, Shoes, Outerwear			
Gifts and Donations			
Children's Activities			
Vet Bills			
Travel, Vacations and Family Fun			
Self-Improvement & Hobbies			
Computer/Electronics			
Holiday Pay (if self-employed)			
Other			
Total Lump Sum and Annual Expenses			
TOTAL EXPENSES			

CASH FLOW SURPLUS (DEFICIT):			

Either way, you can also see how your spending habits line up with your goals. If you see that more money flows out to the cable company than to your RSPS, you might want to ask yourself if Seinfeld will foot the bill for your retirement home.

IN REVIEWING your worksheet, here are some serious questions to ask yourself:

· Are you spending more than you earn?
· Are you spending or allocating enough money for your goals?
· Does it show that there's money left over at the end of the month when you know there isn't? (If so, what did you forget to include? Do you make two loan payments a month and only account for one? Did you include car insurance? Gifts? Clothes? Travel?)
· Does your spending reflect your values and what's important to you?
· Are you saving enough to see you through an emergency?
· Are you saving for retirement?

Once you have an accurate picture of what's coming in and what's going out, you may be surprised by how easy it is to find ways to make simple changes that have massive impacts.

The first step in the *Spending and Savings Plan* exercise was to show you your current spending patterns. The next step is to become more proactive in planning how you want to spend your money going forward. It's good to know how you have been spending your money lately, but it's more important to decide how you want to spend your money next month and the month after that.

LAURA AND MARK knew they were sinking but were afraid to face it. When they filled in the *Spending and Savings Plan* worksheet, they saw in black and white that every month they were spending $1,000 more than they were bringing in.

If they had kept their head in the sand, each year they would have sunk another $12,000 in debt.

Laura and Mark had to face facts. They could either cut their expenses or earn more money. They liked the life they were building, so instead of cutting back they were inspired to earn more.

The next month Mark landed a great job that increased his salary by $30,000! After taxes, he took home $18,000 more per year—more than they needed to live the life they loved.

Filling out the *Spending and Savings Plan* didn't make Mark any more capable of getting the higher-paying job. But the information, coupled with the desire to live the life they wanted, was a powerful motivator.

What's scary is that their fear of facing the numbers could have cost them $12,000 a year in debt and $18,000 in lost revenue.

MUCH OF WHAT we do with clients involves exploring life choices and trade-offs:
- If you bought a bigger house, what would that look like in terms of finances?
- If you start a family, how will that change current spending and future plans?
- If you retire early but start that new business you've always dreamed about, what will your financial life look like?

We're not saying that it's easy to make trade-off decisions and to limit spending. We live in a material culture, one in which we constantly get subtle (and not-so-subtle) messages that we should have everything we want and to use credit if we don't have the cash today. However, by looking at your priorities and the financial impact under different scenarios, you can make better life and financial decisions that consider both your current and future lifestyle needs.

Turning the Numbers into Conscious Choices

There are a lot of things you have to spend money on. Take the financial pressure off by having a plan that reflects your financial realities and your financial goals.

Review your goals to remind yourself what really matters to you. And be real. If completing your *Spending and Savings Plan* has reminded you of goals or values that you didn't write down before, go back to your goals sheet and add them now.

Maybe seeing how much you have been spending on renovations helped you realize that a beautiful and secure home is a big part of your best life. If so, write it down as a goal and set an annual dollar value for renovations on your goals sheet. If, on the other hand, you hate that you spend more on faucets than on a goal that really matters to you, it will be easier for you to choose to spend less at the home improvement store from now on.

Review your expenses line by line. Have a good look at where you're spending your money and ask yourself: "Is this expense necessary? Could I do better? Is it really important to me?" Likely you'll be surprised by how much you're spending in some categories without even noticing.

Review your income. Is it time to ask for the raise they've been hinting about? Is there a way to bring in some additional income through overtime, a part-time job, renting out a room in your house?

Now watch yourself spend money. Every time you spend, ask yourself: "Am I moving one step closer to my goal? Or one step farther away? Do I really want this? Or do I want something else more?"

You deserve to live your best life. When you see ways to achieve your goals, you will inevitably start to see your spending decrease and your savings for your goals increase. The answer to "how" will become obvious because you'll be motivated by your goals.

SHEILA AND DAVID have travel as a top-priority goal, and are always trying to find ways to put more in their travel fund. Sheila explains: "Every month we set aside $300 for a big trip—this year it was the Arizona desert, next year it's Hawaii—and another $100 for short jaunts to Whistler, and trips to visit family in eastern Canada.

Recently we realized that if we could just find another $60 a month, we could squeeze in a whole extra trip each year. We reviewed our *Spending and Savings Plan*, looking for something that we could cut by $60. It didn't take long to spot that this was exactly what we were paying our housekeeper.

David and I will quite happily take turns vacuming to get an extra weekend away."

Consciously Create a Spending and Savings Plan

If you can't afford your goals *and* your lifestyle in your current *Spending and Savings Plan*, you'll need to make some changes to help you use your money to your best advantage.

Open yourself up to seeing what financial changes you can make, so that you can start living the life you want with the money you have. What would better reflect your goals and values? What changes would free up money for the things that matter? What would it take to gain control?

What Can I Change?

Use the third column in the *Spending and Savings Plan* to make a note of the income or expense areas you might be able to change to improve the bottom line. See if you can free up more money to break-even, pay off more to debt or start to save for the things you want.

Your *Spending and Savings Plan* should reflect your goals and values and should be moving you forward towards the lifestyle and goals that you want. As you work through your plan and become more conscious of how you spend and bring money into your life, you will find in time you might be able to put more and more money towards your priority goals.

Use your instincts to guide you to make the necessary changes, and for a little extra guidance, use the hints that follow.

You will likely go over your *Spending and Savings Plan* a few times before you settle on numbers that work for you, so use pencil, stay open, and start your plan.

Hints on Setting Reasonable Targets

Plan to spend less than you earn. Keep that basic principle in mind as you create your plan. If you're currently overspending every month, start by looking for ways to cut back. If you can imagine spending less on gasoline and parking by carpooling, make that part of your plan—write it down.

Plan for your goals. If you have a goal to start art classes, fill in the amount you need to set aside each month on your *Spending and Savings Plan* to reach your goal. If you also have a goal to buy a townhouse and you need to save for a down payment, then add another line to set aside money for your house goal. Your goals are central to your plan; you have to eat but you also have to have money for your goals. This is where you start to think about how you can make that happen.

Plan to have fun. Your financial plan won't work if you feel too constrained. The point is to free up money for the things that matter and sometimes going out with your friends matters— so don't forget to allocate some money for fun.

And don't feel guilty about spending this money—enjoy it—it's just as much a part of your plan, and just as important, as paying down debt. The key is to really enjoy spending the money you have allocated, and not to spend a penny more.

Plan to give a little to get a little. Say you want to increase your savings by $50 a month. That money has to come from somewhere. As you write it down on your plan, decide what area you can shave by $50 and make that change on your plan as well. Can you brown bag it and start packing your lunch or drink your coffee at home in the morning? Can you be more careful at the grocery store and cut back that monthly expense? Thinking in terms of give-and-take will help you make a plan, and it will also help you stick to it.

Plan to stop worrying. If you create a *Spending and Savings Plan* that covers your needs and your goals, you will know exactly how much money you have to spend on things. So what's to worry about? You will know how much you can spend on haircuts and you will have decided that it's okay. Your job is then to stick to the plan, and remember why you will stick to the plan—so you can meet your goals and enjoy your life.

You will know how much you are saving for retirement and that you are on track. You will know that you have budgeted for car repairs and debt repayment and that one doesn't have to preclude the other.

Plan so that choices are easy. If your brother asks you to join him for a ski weekend, you won't have to worry about whether or not you can afford it. If you have an expense line for travel, you will know what you planned to spend on travel and you will know if a ski weekend fits in with those plans. Better still, if it's a smidgen over budget, and it's important to you, you will know how to go back over the plan and choose something to cut back on to free up some cash for the trip. And if it isn't in the plan, you can tell him that it isn't in your plan. Full stop. It's your money—your life!

Plan to have more breathing room in the future. All things in good time. If things are tight now, don't despair. Be creative about increasing your income so that you can expand your spending and savings in the future. If you plan for it, you can have room to maneuver.

Be patient: it may take several months to get your *Spending and Savings Plan* where you want it to be, so keep coming back to it and tweaking it where you can.

Be Prepared for Change
Now you have a *Net Worth Statement* that reflects your financial starting point and a *Spending and Savings Plan* that reflects your values.

You will continually need to fine-tune your choices to create a balance between living the lifestyle you want today and planning for your future.

You might find that the amount of money you thought you needed and the amount you actually need changes. So make adjustments. Just make sure that when you make changes, you stay on course.

Ideally, you will review your *Net Worth* annually and your *Spending and Savings Plan* periodically throughout the year. Challenge yourself—if you're consistently overspending in one area ask yourself if you need to change your plan or your behaviour, or both. If you're consistently underspending, ask yourself the same questions. This will empower you to make choices *and changes* with confidence.

▸ 8 ◂

|||||||||||||||||||||||||

ON TRACK
MONEY MANAGEMENT
SYSTEM

Annual income twenty pounds, annual expenditure
nineteen pounds nineteen and six, result happiness.
Annual income twenty pounds, annual expenditure
twenty pounds ought and six, result misery.

CHARLES DICKENS

ONCE YOU'VE COMPLETED your *Spending and Savings Plan*
worksheet so that, at least on paper, you're living within your
means and saving for your goals, you need to make sure you
can stick with the program.

Budget Blues

Meticulously measured budgets and long tallies of receipts
are not the answer for everyone. If you have the patience
and discipline to do that, you probably already know where
every penny is going so you don't need a system to get your
cash flow on track. We're often asked about the best account-
ing or budgeting software to keep track of expenses, such as
Quicken or Microsoft Money. Honestly, we're not big fans of
any budgeting software.

The trouble is most people don't use their 'money time'
wisely—and often focus their attention on the wrong things
when it comes to budgeting programs. Staying on track with

your money isn't about dumping a whole bunch of numbers into a computer every month and then wasting time juggling those figures. There's a feeling that if you put them all neatly on a spreadsheet, somehow magically the numbers will balance and at the end of the month you won't have spent more than you made.

Of course, we're big advocates of having a good handle on your expenses. The key is to do something useful with the information you've been gathering so diligently about your spending and to figure out what the numbers mean.

Added to that is the fact that the word 'budget' has such negative connotations. It feels restrictive as if somebody is slapping you on the wrist; it's like you can never have any fun. Faced with that prospect, it's no wonder people aren't motivated to live on a budget.

Knowing how and where you spend your money is essential—*before* you put your *Spending and Savings Plan* in place. But finding out after the fact that you overspent in a category is useless information unless you set up a system to modify your future spending behaviour.

The real purpose for knowing how much you are spending is to make sure you're living within your means and to help you plan spending for the year ahead. You also need to know if you are setting enough money aside for important life goals—travel, retirement, children's education, charity or making a difference in the world. If you aren't sure how much you need to save now to reach each of your goals, then have your Money Coach or financial advisor run some projections for you.

How can you tell if you don't account for every cent of what's coming in and what's going out? Well, an easy reality check is to see whether you are paying down debt and starting to save for things you need and want.

If you are living within your means and working towards your goals, then you can monitor your budget by looking at the pace of your debt reduction, the quality of your life on a day-to-day basis and your progress in reaching your goals. Your system is working and you may not need to change it.

However, if you're running up balances on your credit card or line of credit, re-mortgaging your home or never making headway with your goals, then you absolutely need to set up a system to help you stay within the parameters of your *Spending and Savings Plan*

On Track Money Management System

Our *On Track Money Management System* is designed to help you do two things: a) stay on track with monthly and annual expenses; and b) save for your goals.

The system goes back to the old days of putting money into envelopes to make sure everything—from groceries to the gas bill—got paid. When payday rolled around, you'd put cash for groceries in one envelope, money for the bills in another, savings towards new clothes for school in yet another and so on.

To implement our system we suggest opening several bank accounts. Here's what we recommend:
1. One Main Chequing Account for fixed costs and regular monthly payments
2. A Monthly Spending Account for things you tend to spend money on every month
3. Several Savings accounts to save up for Lump Sum and Annual Expenses

Refer back to your *Spending and Savings Plan* and you will see that the Expenses Section has been divided into these three categories.

The idea is to use different bank accounts to create 'electronic' envelopes—so the car insurance money gets saved and not spent on pedicures, the account for university fees adds up instead of being drained by car repairs or other unexpected expenses. And the vacation budget, often a priority but usually the first to be sacrificed to overspending in other areas, gets stashed in an account labelled 'Travel,' safe from impulse shoe buying or unlimited lattes.

In effect, it doesn't just give you a budget to follow, it forces you to limit your spending in each category to the amount you have in the account. If you've determined that it costs you $800 a month for groceries and by the third week you're down to your last $60 in the Monthly Spending Account, no seeking solace in the credit card or pilfering other accounts. Get out the recipes and use up what's left in the cupboard.

CONSIDER THE CASE of Jennifer, a client who confessed to constantly living in her overdraft. "I had no trouble putting together a budget based on what I had spent," she said. "I was spending more than I was bringing in and when annual expenses rolled around, it was a scramble to find the money to pay them.

"But when I started planning ahead for those annual expenses and putting away the money every month so I'd have money to pay them—wow, what a difference it made. No more panic when big annual bills came up and no more running up my credit cards to pay for them."

It took some discussion and hard decisions to set priorities. Jennifer opted for several accounts, because if there was money in a single account that had to cover several long-term items, there was a temptation to borrow from it with the expectation that money would magically appear to fill the account by a bill's due date. Some clients choose to manage with fewer savings accounts, but the key is to create clarity. Do I have money for clothes, or not? Have we spent the dining out money or is there still some left for Friday night?

The payoff can be huge. And not just in terms of money but of peace of mind.

"The first time my annual insurance bill came around and I actually had enough money in a savings account to pay it I realized my plan was working," said Jennifer. "And when I was able to book a vacation and pay for it with my Travel Savings instead of putting it off or putting it onto my credit card, I was thrilled. The spending guilt was gone. Now it's easy to make financial choices—I can walk by Manolo Blahniks on sale and keep walking because I know if I spend money on them, there goes the trip to Hawaii."

ON TRACK MONEY MANAGEMENT SYSTEM

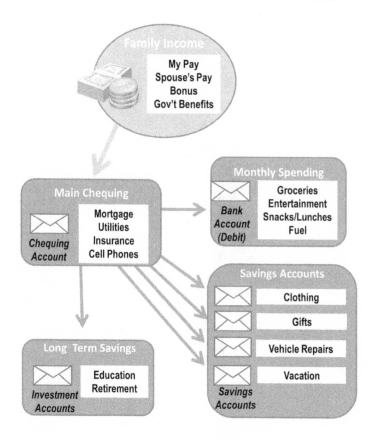

TYPES OF ACCOUNTS
RECOMMENDED FOR THE ON TRACK
MONEY MANAGEMENT SYSTEM

Account	How Many do I need?	Purpose	Type of Bank Account	Features		How do I spend money out of this account?
				Debit Card Access?	Set up Overdraft?	
Main Chequing	One	Fixed Costs - Regular Monthly Payments & Bills (Rent/mortgage, hydro, phone, monthly insurance payments, etc.)	Chequing with unlimited transactions	No	Yes	Pre-authorized payments, bill payments, write cheques
Chequing #2	One	Monthly Spending (Groceries, gas, pet food, dining out, etc.)	Chequing with low fee Depending on how many times you shop, may want to have unlimited transactions	Yes	No	Debit card – point of sale purchases or withdraw cash
Savings	Several	Lump Sum & Annual Expenses (Clothing, gifts, property insurance, vacations, children's activities, etc.)	No fee high-interest savings accounts	No	No	Transfer money to credit card or main chequing account to cover purchases made (eg. Buy clothing for $75.25 with credit card, transfer $75.25 to credit card from Clothing savings account)

Implementing the On Track Money Management System

1. Main Chequing Account

THE GOAL: To separate your bill money from your spending money. Keep only enough in this account to cover your bills and regular monthly payments. This way you don't have to worry about spending the rent or mortgage money on groceries or clothes. The money stays in the Main Chequing Account until the bills need to be paid.

MONTHLY FIXED COSTS are bills and regular payments that are approximately the same amount every month.
· For example: rent, mortgage, phone and cable bills, car loan, newspaper subscription and monthly savings for RESP and RSP payments are all likely to be the same amount each month and thus considered 'fixed.'

THE PLAN
· Use your Main Chequing Account for *monthly fixed costs.*
· Deposit all income into your Main Chequing Account.
· Pay bills and expenses that are fixed and payable monthly from this account.
· Leave only enough money in this account to cover your bills and fixed costs for the month. You will find your total for your monthly fixed costs on your *Spending and Savings Plan.*
· Don't use this account for spending money; it's just for the bills.
· Leave a small buffer of say $50 to $100 per month to cover any variances in the bills.
· Take out overdraft protection on this account, but only use it in an absolute emergency.

TIPS
· You may want to consider equal billing for utility bills like gas and electricity to help even out your expenses. You can

arrange with the utility companies to pay a set amount every month to eliminate seasonal jumps in your bills. This allows you to more accurately predict your monthly costs.

· If you are self-employed we recommend setting up a separate chequing account to use for your business income and expenses. This will keep your business cash flow separate from your personal. To draw money from the business account we recommend transferring a regular pay or 'salary' to your personal account to mimic a paycheque. The amount must be fixed and drawn consistently i.e. once a month, 15th and 30th or every two weeks.

· If you are self-employed you also need to save for your 'holiday pay' to cover for your loss of income when away from work. This amount should be enough to cover your draw or 'salary' so you can continue to pay your bills and stick to your *Spending and Savings Plan* when you take time off.

2. Monthly Spending Account

THE GOAL: To keep your monthly spending within the limits that you set out in your *Spending and Savings Plan*. Open a second chequing account and give yourself a certain amount each pay period to spend on expenses that you know you will incur every month but want to keep to a specific amount to stay on track. You can spend what's in the account, but when it's gone, it's gone. Plan to cover all the expenses you need and want for each month and no more.

MONTHLY SPENDING includes expenses that you spend money on *every* month, but the amounts can be variable.

For example: You will likely need money every month for groceries, cleaning supplies, gas, bus, parking, entertainment, dining out and spending money but the amount you spend can vary from month to month.

- Use a second chequing account for Monthly Spending.
- The amount you have budgeted for monthly spending expenses can be found on your *Spending and Savings Plan*.
- Transfer this amount of money from your Main Chequing Account each payday.
- Use debit to access this account for your spending.
- This is your spending money for the month, make it last.
- Decline overdraft protection on this account so that when the account is empty, you have to stop spending.

TIP

Transfer half the monthly amount needed on the 15th and 30th or every two weeks if you are paid bi-weekly. We find that two weeks is about as far out as people can plan with their monthly expenses. If you aren't able to stick to your plan and the money is spent in the first week, don't despair— there will be more transferred into your account within two weeks to keep you going for the rest of the month.

SUE AND BOB'S planned monthly spending totalled $1,200. They transfer $600 per pay to their Monthly Spending Account. Their goal is to make this money last for two weeks. If they run out of money in the first week, it's rice and beans till payday.

And yes, Sue does feel like it is a bit limiting to have only so much to spend, but says "it's worth it" as it keeps them from overspending and frees up money for the things they really want, like a trip to Italy.

It works for them and Sue says "Every time I pass over the ice cream aisle I imagine myself sipping a latte on a sidewalk café in Venice!"

3. Savings Accounts—Lump Sum and Annual Expenses
THE GOAL: To set aside an amount every month for the expenses that occur irregularly or annually. By saving monthly

for these expenses you should have the money available when you need it. This way you won't have to rely on credit cards or your line of credit when these expenses come up.

By having a separate account for each type of expense, you will know how much money you have available to spend in each category. It also keeps the money separate from your other spending so you don't accidentally spend your savings on something like dining out or lattes.

LUMP SUM AND ANNUAL EXPENSES are those irregular expenses that come up once a year or sporadically throughout the year.

For example: Car repairs, property taxes, house insurance, clothes, gifts, travel, and vet bills are all things you may need or want to spend money on sometime throughout the year.

THE PLAN
- Review your *Spending and Savings Plan* for expenses that you have planned for in the Savings Accounts—Lump Sum and Annual Expenses section.
- Set up separate high-interest, no-fee savings accounts at your bank for each expense category that you want to save for.
- *Nickname* the accounts for the various expenses you need and want to save for.
- Divide the annual total you planned on spending in each category by the number of paydays you have in a year.
- Transfer this amount to the designated accounts each payday from your Main Chequing Account.
- Debit is usually unavailable on high-interest savings accounts, so when you make a purchase, you can access the funds in one of two ways:

   1. **Pay by Credit Card** and then pay off the credit card immediately from the designated savings account.

Your credit card balance will be at zero (where we like to keep it) and the savings account balance is up to date with the remaining funds available for your next purchase.

2. Pay by Cheque and then transfer the money from the designated savings account to your Main Chequing Account. The money should stay safe in the Main Chequing Account until the cheque is cashed, as this account is not for spending.

TIPS

· When paying off the credit card for a lump sum or annual expense pay the exact amount you spent (e.g., $128.04) so that when the bills come it is easy to see which expenses have been paid for from the designated accounts, and which may have been missed.

· If your bank charges a fee to pay bills from your high-interest savings account it is better to transfer the amount first to your Main Chequing Account. Then pay the credit card bill from the Main Chequing Account as this account should have unlimited transactions. Transfers between accounts should be free.

Fixed Lump Sum and Annual Expenses
These can include all your annual expenses that have a fixed amount due each year. Since the amount for each bill is set, you can tally up all the costs that fit into this category and save for them in one account. Add up the totals and divide by your number of pay periods and start setting the money aside. If you get the timing right the money will be set aside in the account when each bill comes due.

ANNUAL OR LUMP SUM
EXPENSES WORKSHEET

- Make a list of the annual or lump sum expenses you need or want to save for
- Tally up how much you think you will need or want to spend on these expenses in the next 12 months
- Divide the annual amount by the number of pay periods you have in a year (24 pay periods if you are paid on the 15th and 30th of the month or 26 pay periods if you are paid every two weeks)
- Set aside this amount each pay day to save for the things you need and want throughout the year
- See the next page for more detailed information about these expenses.

	Estimated Amount Needed Per Year	Amount to Set Aside Each Payday
FIXED LUMP SUM AND ANNUAL EXPENSES		
Property taxes	$_____	$_____
Vehicle insurance	$_____	$_____
Property Insurance	$_____	$_____
Clubs & Memberships (if paid annually)	$_____	$_____
Magazine Subscriptions	$_____	$_____
Costco Membership/Credit Card Fees	$_____	$_____
Professional / Accounting Fees	$_____	$_____

Total Fixed Lump Sum and Annual Expenses
(these can all be saved for in one account)

	$		$

	Estimated Amount Needed Per Year	Amount to Set Aside Each Payday
VARIABLE LUMP SUM AND ANNUAL EXPENSES *(set up a separate account for each category needed)*		
HOME REPAIRS, FURNITURE, HOUSEHOLD ITEMS	$_____	$_____
VEHICLE REPAIRS AND MAINTENANCE	$_____	$_____
MEDICAL /DENTAL /GLASSES / CONTACTS	$_____	$_____
PERSONAL CARE	$_____	$_____
CLOTHING, SHOES, OUTERWEAR	$_____	$_____
GIFTS AND DONATIONS	$_____	$_____
CHILDREN'S ACTIVITIES	$_____	$_____
VET BILLS	$_____	$_____
TRAVEL, VACATIONS AND FAMILY FUN	$_____	$_____
SELF IMPROVEMENT OR HOBBIES	$_____	$_____
COMPUTER/ELECTRONICS	$_____	$_____
HOLIDAY PAY (If Self Employed)	$_____	$_____
OTHER: _____	$_____	$_____
OTHER: _____	$_____	$_____
OTHER: _____	$_____	$_____

Variable Lump Sum and Annual Expenses

Home Repairs or Major Purchases—renovations, painting, new furniture, stereo, lamps, sheets, curtains... How much do you need, or can you afford, to allocate to these types of expenses?

Car Repairs and Maintenance—include regular scheduled maintenance as well as things like new brakes, new tires, and the deductible on break-ins or car repairs from an accident.

Medical/Dental/Glasses/Contacts—if you have to pay for all or some of these expenses irregularly, start setting the money aside now. Don't forget massage, chiropractic, naturopath and physio.

Personal Care—if you have large expenses for hair, makeup or other personal care items, save monthly so the money is available when you need it.

Clothes—if you tend to do a few big shops per year it's nice to save up so you have the money before you go shopping. Then you know how much you can spend.

Gifts—Birthdays, Mother's Day, Father's Day, anniversary, Christmas, weddings, new babies, house warmings... Write out a schedule of holidays, birthdays and other miscellaneous events you buy gifts for. This could include expenses for family gatherings or birthday parties you host.

Children's Activities—List all the activities for your children and the associated costs throughout the year. Include amounts for summer camps, school trips, sports activities and equipment, music lessons, drama class etc.

Vet Bills—Plan for the costs of the annual checkup and regular shots plus the unexpected vet bill that may come up.

Travel—Include major vacations, trips back home, camping, weekend getaways etc. Set aside money monthly (and extra when you can) so there is money for these much-needed breaks. But remember, the rule is you can only spend what's in the account, so if there is only $549 in the travel account, it is a $549 vacation.

Self-Improvement or Hobbies—this can include anything from French classes, to yoga or photography to counseling or a course you might need to take for work.

Time off or Holiday Pay—If you are self-employed you also need to save for your 'holiday pay' to cover for your loss of income when away from work.

Are There Goals You Want to Start Saving For?

After you've finished taking care of all your regular expenses, are there other goals you want to start to save for? Maybe you want to save for a home, a new car, a major trip, retirement—your list may not be the same as your friend's or your neighbours. It is as individual as you are.

Start saving a certain amount each payday. Even if you can only save $25 per month, just get started with whatever you can, working towards increasing that amount whenever possible. Depending on your goals and how much you think you can save, pick two or three of your major goals and start saving for them every month.

KARIN GOT SERIOUS about her goal once she named her account.

"For years I've heard Sheila teach people to set up bank accounts with nicknames for their goals. To be honest, I thought it was a little hokey!

"But a few years ago my husband and I started thinking seriously about buying a property on Salt Spring Island. We had some savings that we could allocate to it, so I thought I'd give Sheila's idea a try. I set up a high-interest savings account, named the account "Salt Spring Home" put $3,000 into the fund and started making monthly transfers.

"I kid you not, within three months of opening the account, we found a property on Salt Spring, put in an offer, found the rest of the down payment money and bought a fantastic house, way before we ever imagined we would. I'm convinced that by giving the savings account a name and putting money into the account, we put out a very strong message that we were committed to our dream. So, what are you ready to make happen?"

FAQs and Objections

I don't want too many accounts:
If you only use one account and the money you need for irregular or lump sum expenses is in your chequing account, you might continue using your debit card or writing cheques until the money is gone. Then when the expenses come due, you won't have money to pay them

Or if you only have one savings account then it will not be clear how much money is available for clothes or gifts at any one time. And what if you spend all the savings on travel? Then there isn't anything left for the vet bill when it comes due.

Clarity is key. Having several separate accounts can help you make decisions about what you can—and can't—afford.

Why can't I put car repairs and home repairs in one account?
Car repairs are generally not discretionary. When the car breaks down you need to get it fixed. It's important to always have some money in this account, just in case you need it.

Many home repairs are more discretionary such as new hardwood floors. If you were saving money for both car and home repairs in the same account there is a danger you might spend the amount set aside for car repairs on home expenses.

Then when the car does have its inevitable breakdown you might find that the money was spent on gleaming new floors.

Will it cost me more to open all these accounts?

We don't like to pay bank fees any more than you do, so we try to keep fees to a minimum. We suggest a low monthly fee account for the two chequing accounts you need and no fee savings accounts for the lump sum and annual accounts. Check your bank's website or call the toll-free number to find out more about what type of accounts your bank offers and the fees they charge.

Can I borrow from one account if I'm short?

Many people try to 'borrow' funds from one account if they have overspent in another category. We don't recommend this as it's not as easy as you think to pay it back.

You might also be tempted to 'steal' from an account but that implies you will not be paying the money back. Let's say you overspend on travel and 'steal' money from your clothes account to pay for the great trip you just had. This means you now have less money to spend on clothes. It's your money and your choice, but since there is only so much money to cover all your expenses, make conscious choices whenever you can.

BY FOLLOWING the *On Track Money Management System* you not only achieve your goals, you do so without the stress of incurring debt.

▸9◂

||||||||||||||||||||||||||

DEBT:
THE GOOD, THE BAD
AND THE UGLY

The price of anything is the amount of life you exchange for it.
HENRY THOREAU

WE MET SUSAN at The Money Map, a workshop program that we offer through Money Coaches Canada. She came to the course hoping to get her debt under control and to learn more about investing so she could retire early. She worked diligently on a *Spending and Savings Plan* that would cover her current needs and at the same time put her on track to clearing her debt and investing for retirement.

Susan was delighted that she had a plan and felt she could take the next steps on her own. The problem was that she couldn't make her plan work. Instead of returning to a zero balance each month, her credit card ballooned and it wasn't long before Susan was ready to turn to the solution she had relied on in the past—running up her line of credit to pay off her credit card debt. And then the cycle would start again.

Susan realized she needed help and hired us to see what had gone wrong. She had all kinds of explanations for the discrepancy in what she planned to spend—on clothes, eating out and other discretionary spending—and what she actually spent. Her closet was overflowing, she planned vacations she couldn't afford, she redid her living room but none of it brought her the happiness she was seeking.

Susan is not alone. Living within your means can seem almost like a quaint old-fashioned notion. Look to the United States and its sub-prime mortgage debacle—the so-called NINJA loans, No Income, No Job or Assets and more often than not, still approved!

THESE DAYS governments regularly run up massive debts and we frequently hear news of one country or another facing a credit crunch. The United States was brought to the edge of a debt crisis and it is by no means certain it will avoid that forever. Perhaps it should come as no surprise that so many people are overspending—it's like living beyond our means has become the new 'normal'.

Debt is a huge problem for Canadians as well, a problem that is only getting worse as the economic downturn continues to reverberate through the lives of ordinary working people. Canadians' household debt has risen to record highs compared to our disposable income and there is no sign of that reversing. More than half a million Canadians are behind on their credit payments. More and more Canadians are using their credit cards and lines of credit to finance day-to-day expenditures and the bills are starting to add up. The total national household debt in Canada has been at an all-time high.

It may be easy to understand why we're in the debt mess, but not so easy to find a way out. If you are in debt yourself, you might be hoping that the debt problem will resolve itself by some miraculous bonus cheque or inheritance. Or you might be avoiding the issue because you just can't see yourself getting out of the debt cycle no matter what you do.

WHILE AVOIDING the discomfort of dealing with debt may be easier in the short run, the stress and anxiety caused by not dealing with debt can lead to feelings of shame or fear and to serious arguments with your spouse and family. Some people try to 'fix' the problems themselves, but ingrained habits die hard. An honest look at the numbers and a proven system with accountability and professional support has worked for many of our clients. Clients are often amazed at how quickly their situation has turned around once they were truly committed to making changes with their money.

A good place to start is by understanding the type of debt you have.

Debt: The Good, the Bad and the Ugly

The less debt you have the better. That being said, you will hear people talking about good debt versus bad debt. Put simply:

Good debt is used to purchase an asset, like a house or investments. And ideally these are appreciating assets, something with real value that you could sell if you needed to clear the debt. So while a car loan has an asset attached to it, it is depreciating, so something to be cautious about.

Bad debt comes from buying 'stuff' and living beyond your means. If you are running a balance on your line of credit or your credit card that originated from purchases that you didn't have the money for, this would be bad debt.

Ugly debt can be either good or bad debt spinning out of control. If you aren't sure how much debt you have, if you have balances on multiples credit cards, or if you are using your line of credit to pay off your credit card or your mortgage then take a deep breath, get honest with yourself, sharpen your pencil and make a payback plan before it's too late.

When interest rates are low, people talk about 'cheap money.' You might be tempted to take on debt now because you think it won't cost you as much as when interest rates are higher. Maybe, but if you aren't financially or emotionally prepared with a plan to pay down your debt, you need to remember that overdue payments, damage to your credit, sleepless nights, stress and lack of freedom all add to the cost of borrowing.

IT MAY BE necessary to incur debt to attain your goals (e.g., a mortgage for a house). That's okay. The key is that you stay in control of your debt, that you have a plan to pay it off—and you stick to it.

Responsible Debt Management

Borrowing has become a way of life. Our buy-now-pay-later culture seems to accept debt, and the costs associated with it, as part of the cost of living. It is important to remember that although nearly half of Canadian families spend more than they earn, the flip side to that statistic is that more than half don't. You need to decide for yourself how comfortable you are with debt and credit and not be swayed by what the Joneses are up to. (You never know how well they sleep at night, do you?)

Stores and businesses have made having credit a necessary convenience. Even if you don't think of it as borrowing, you are using your credit when you pay in installments on your insurance, or use your credit card to automatically pay your phone bill or reserve a hotel room. There's nothing wrong with taking advantage of these conveniences, so long as you do it responsibly.

Given the interest rates they can charge, creditors today are all too happy to lend money. If you get credit card offers in the mail every week, it's not because they think you're special. Creditors make lots and lots of money from people who are sloppy at paying their bills, or who buy into the idea that paying a little interest is a cost of living.

If you can't pay off your credit card each month, don't use credit.

There's no question, using your credit card is a convenient way to shop or buy things online. And as long as you pay off the balance each month by the due date, there's no problem. However if you aren't able to, the clock starts ticking on with interest charges from the moment you make your purchase. Beware—if you can't pay off the balance by the due date it means you don't have the money to cover the purchases you made in the first place.

Your Line of Credit isn't your money.

Bank statements and Internet banking sites often make your line of credit look like any other account. Instead of having warning lights flashing, "This is money you owe us!" they often start off with, "Your available balance is..." It is a nuance that costs some people a lot of money. Don't treat your line of credit (or your overdraft) like any other chequing or savings account. It's not your money.

These accounts are bridging or emergency resources only, and because they usually have a competitive interest rate, they can be very useful for those purposes. If your kitchen sink springs a leak while you are at work and you come home to find the downstairs neighbour has called a very expensive plumber who only deals in cash, you might need to draw some cash from your line of credit. Okay, but when you use it, remember that it is a loan and you want to put a plan in place to pay it back.

When you use credit wisely (and by that we mean you pay your bills in full and on time every month) you amplify your life choices. You build a solid credit history and you demonstrate your financial control. All you have to do is make sure you have cash in the bank to cover your monthly loan payments and anything *and everything* you put on credit.

Don't rely on a lender to tell you what you can, or can't afford.
You might be surprised by how much money lenders are willing to offer you. If you ask your bank or mortgage broker for a mortgage pre-approval, you are likely to be approved for more than you think you can afford because lenders apply generic formulas to your income, debt load and credit history. They don't know all the details of your monthly expenses.

If you don't think you can handle the loan payments associated with a purchase, trust your gut and your plan. Lenders may not know what other goals you are working to achieve.

Borrow only what you need, and what you can foreseeably pay back. If lenders offer you more, great. You can still walk out with the amount of money you choose and the knowledge that even in the face of temptation, you chose to protect your future, and your sanity, by not taking on more than you can handle.

Get Out of Debt

No matter what the reason for the debt, so-called 'good' or 'bad,' debt limits your options. It is as simple as that.

When you owe money, you usually have to make principal payments and interest payments monthly. That commits a significant portion of your income and limits your choices. Nothing causes more stress than being stuck in a job you hate because you need the paycheque to service your debt load.

Buy yourself the freedom you deserve. Don't think of debt payment as punishment or you'll hate paying it. Taking control is about opening up possibilities. Paying off debt is a really good thing.

The first step is to be sure that you're not continuing to add to your debt. If you have been able to put together a *Spending and Savings Plan* that now shows a surplus (or at least a break-even), and have successfully implemented the *On Track Money Management System*, you're well on your way to breaking the patterns that may have been the source of the debt in the first place.

Now all you need to do is to work on the debt you've accumulated to date.

10 Tips to Get Out and Stay Out of Debt

1. **Know why you want to be Debt-Free.** The bigger and more inspiring the "why," the easier the "how" will become. Use your "why" as the motivation, the light at the end of the tunnel, the reason you are going to work hard or smarter to get out of debt. Imagine how good it will feel to be debt-free and the freedom or choices you will have once you are out of debt.

2. **Make paying down debt a #1 priority.** Consciously make an effort to pay down debt each month. You can take control. Making paying down debt a #1 priority doesn't mean it's the only priority you have, but it does have to be a priority because it's not going to happen on its own. You might have credit cards and lines of credit that are just sort of revolving—you pay them down, you run them up, you pay them down and run them up so you feel like you're doing something about the debt, but in actual fact you're not making any progress at all. Or you might just be paying the interest on your line of credit, but nothing towards the principal. We like to call this the 'never-never plan' because unless you start making extra payments, the debt will never be paid off. Think about how you are using your credit cards and line of credit and make it a priority to pay down your debt.

3. **Make debt reduction systematic.** Decide on a fixed amount you will pay each month (or per payday) towards your debt, then set this up as an automatic payment with your bank. By making the payment automatic there will be no debate

or wiggle room when it comes to paying the amount you decided on. You'll know your system is working when you see your debt and your stress steadily decrease.

4. **Keep a running tally of your debt.** Track the balance on your debt each month. Make sure it is going down, not just staying the same. When you see it go down, you'll think twice about racking it back up. If you have several different debts—credit cards, a line of credit, student loans—take a tally of them at a given point in time during the month, let's say on the first of the month. Track your balances at the beginning of the month, and then again at the beginning of the next month and see if your debt has gone up or down. This will keep you honest and show how much progress you've made or whether you need to revisit your spending habits.

5. **Shop around for a lower interest rate.** Reduce your interest rate by all means. Don't reduce your commitment to be debt-free. You may be carrying a balance on your credit cards at rates up to 19% to 25% or more so see if you can get a lower rate on your credit cards or perhaps transfer the balance to a line of credit to reduce your interest costs.

6. **Tackle one debt at a time.** Throwing $100 a month at five different debts can cost you money and momentum. You won't see any serious progress; meanwhile you are paying interest on everything. Put the majority of your resources into one debt and make the minimum payments on everything else. You will feel great when you can cross the first debt off your list, then move on to the next.

7. **Pay down the debt with the highest interest rate first.** The sooner you can get rid of high-interest credit cards and debt, the more progress you'll make.

8. **Pay off your credit cards in full each month. If you can't:**
   - Stop using your credit cards; it may be the only way. Start using cash. If you don't trust yourself with a credit card, simply put the credit card away and remove the temptation.
   - BUT I really NEED to use my credit card! If you really have to use your credit card, after you make the purchase, go online and transfer the money from your bank to your credit card immediately. This way even though you have used your credit card, the balance will be paid off before you get the bill. And the rule is you can only use the credit card if you have money in the bank to pay it off immediately.
   - It's best to use one credit card that has a zero balance, then if for any reason you forget to pay off your recent expense the evidence will be apparent when you get your statement. To stay on track, you must pay off this credit card every month to keep the balance at zero. If you don't have the money to pay off the card when the statement comes, you'll need to find it (and this may mean emptying your much-cherished travel fund to pay for your overzealous spending).

9. **Consolidate all debt to one loan or line of credit at the lowest possible rate.** This will reduce your interest charges significantly, but be careful: this only works if you are truly ready to make a change to your spending and have a plan not to run up your debt again. If you continue to use your credit cards irresponsibly or without a clear plan (and commitment) to pay them off each month you'll dig yourself deeper in the hole. So don't consolidate your loans until you have proven to yourself that your financial thinking and your financial habits have changed for good. Have a clear plan before you consolidate and make this the last time that you ever consolidate debts.

10. **Set a date to be debt-free.** When you know the date, you can see the end. Setting a date for when you want to be debt-free

will help put an action plan in place and get your butt in gear to make it happen. Once you review the numbers and the goal, for instance, "I have $24,000 in debt and want to be debt-free in one year," you will then have to ask yourself: "Am I prepared to do what it takes to make this happen?" Or is this goal a little too optimistic and needing review? Don't underestimate yourself. Once the goal is set you'll be surprised at how creative you can be in doing what it takes to meet your goal once you are committed to it.

KYLE AND SHARON are in their 40s. Ten years ago they bought a house, had two children soon after, and before they knew it their debt load ran up to almost $50,000. It's stressful for them and has caused countless arguments. They believe they have stopped adding to debt but the amount they have accumulated feels staggering to them. They try to pay about $1,000 to their debt each month, but the balances never seem to go down.

The children are now five and eight. With the youngest in school they no longer have large daycare costs and feel it's time to really tackle their debt and find a way to get out and stay out of debt. But how to do it, and where to start? They have tried before and it hasn't worked. They decided they need professional help so they hired us to get them working together and out of debt.

We took a closer look at their statements to see what was happening. In turns out yes, indeed they were paying about $1,000 each month towards debt, but they were also still using their credit cards for things like gas, clothing, gifts and the occasional car repair. They also had a few of their bills automatically charged to their credit cards.

By paying down $1,000 per month they felt like they should be making progress but they were not paying attention to the new amounts they were billing to their cards each

Debt, in Order of Repayment Priority	Outstanding Balance	Interest Rate %	Credit Limit	Interest Per Year	Min. Monthly Payment
1. MasterCard—Joint	$3,000	24.99	$5,000	$750	$90
2. Visa—Kyle	$4,850	19.99	$5,000	$970	$146
3. Visa—Sharon	$5,500	19.99	$7,500	$1,099	$165
4. MasterCard—Kyle	$9,900	5.90	$10,000	$584	$297
5. Line of Credit (LOC)	$26,500	3.50	$30,000	$928	$77
TOTAL DEBT	**$49,750**		**$57,500**	**$4,331**	**$775**

month. Most months, they were actually charging more than $1,000 to their credit cards but still making payments of only $1,000 per month. This behaviour is what led to the slow creeping up of their balances over the last 10 years.

Here's what we recommended to Kyle and Sharon:

1. Set up the *On Track Money Management System.*
   - Review all expenses clearly and determine how much you can truly afford to put towards debt.
   - Set clear parameters for what you can spend on discretionary items like dining out, gifts and travel.
   - Save ahead for the expenses you plan to make throughout the year for summer camps, travel and car repairs.

2. Pay off the joint MasterCard with the Line of Credit (LOC).
   - By moving this small, but high-interest debt to your LOC at 3.5% you will save about $645 in interest per year.
   - This also frees up one credit card with a zero balance.

3. Only use your joint MasterCard.
   - It may seem crazy to use this card with an interest rate of 24.99% *but*, now that the balance is at zero, the goal is to

keep it at zero and pay off this card in full, every month by the due date.

- The interest rate is irrelevant as you will not pay any interest costs if you pay off the balance in full each month.
- Use this card responsibly—if you pay for things like summer camps, or flights back home, first make sure you have saved the money in the appropriate accounts so you can pay off the credit card as soon as you use it.
- Once the debt is more in check, shop around for a better rate on a joint credit card.

4. Next, tackle one debt at a time.
- Focus on paying off Kyle's Visa next. With a balance of $4,850 at 19.99% it has the next highest interest rate and the smallest balance.
- With a realistic *Spending and Savings Plan* in place and daycare costs now eliminated, you have $1,400 per month to apply towards your debt.
- Pay $861 per month on Kyle's Visa and the minimum payment on all the other debts
- At this rate, Kyle's Visa will be paid out in six months.
- Next tackle Sharon's Visa by paying $1,026 per month to this card (the $165 minimum you were paying on this card plus the $861 freed up from Kyle's credit card payment).
- At this rate Sharon's Visa will be paid out in 12 months. Move to repaying the next debt using the same system until all your debts are repaid.

5. Use our Debt-Free Calculator to calculate your Debt-Free Date
- Our Debt-Free Calculator prioritizes your debt repayment schedule and shows when you will be debt-free. *(see example on the next page)*
- If you stick to this plan you will pay off your debt in just over three years.

KYLE AND SHARON are thrilled at the thought of being debt-free (other than their mortgage) after struggling for so long. It feels liberating to them to actually imagine what they could do with all the money they will have freed up when their debts are paid. They might even be able to retire at 60 after all.

Now instead of arguing over the bills each month they hold a money meeting to work together to stay on track and to use their new skills and motivation to retire debt-free by 60. Throw in a glass of wine and it becomes a fun meeting to build a life together based on their priorities and plan for their future.

When's Your Debt Free Date?

Monthly Payment Available	$1,400				
Credit Card or Loan Name	MC - Joint	Visa - Kyle	Visa - Sharon	MC - Kyle	MC - K
Debt Repayment Order	1	2	3	4	5
Balance of Debt	$0	$4,850	$5,500	$9,900	$29,500
Promotional Rate	0.00%	0.00%	0.00%	0.00%	
# Months at Promotional Rate	0	0	0	0	
Current Interest Rate (or Fixed after promo)	24.99%	19.99%	19.99%	5.90%	3.50%
Minimum Required Payment	$0.00	$146.00	$165.00	$297.00	$77.00

When's Your Debt Free Date?	
Initial Debt	$49,750
Accelerated Payment	$715
Month out of Debt	39
Total Debt Payments	$53,840
Total Interest Paid	$4,090
Debt Free Date	Jan-2016

Start Month	Start Year			MC - Joint		Visa - Kyle		Visa - Sharon		MC - Kyle		MC - K		Total
Oct	2012			$0		$4,850		$5,500		$9,900		$29,500		Balance
				0.00%		0.00%		0.00%		0.00%		0.00%		of all
				0		0		0		0		0		Loans
				24.99%		19.99%		19.99%		5.90%		3.50%		
				$0		$146		$165		$297		$77		

Date	Extra Payment	Notes	Month	Payment	Balance	Payment	Balance	Payment	Balance	Payment	Balance	Payment	Balance	Month
Oct-2012	$0	Transferred Joint MC to LOC	0		$0		$4,850		$5,500		$9,900		$29,500	0
Nov-2012	$0		1	$0	$0	$861	$4,070	$165	$5,427	$297	$9,652	$77	$29,509	1
Dec-2012	$0		2	$0	$0	$861	$3,277	$165	$5,352	$290	$9,402	$77	$29,518	2
Jan-2013	$0		3	$0	$0	$861	$2,470	$165	$5,276	$297	$9,151	$77	$29,527	3
Feb-2013	$0		4	$0	$0	$861	$1,650	$165	$5,199	$297	$8,890	$77	$29,536	4
Mar-2013	$0		5	$0	$0	$861	$817	$165	$5,121	$297	$8,645	$77	$29,546	5
Apr-2013	$0		6	$0	$0	$830	$0	$196	$5,010	$297	$8,392	$77	$29,555	6
May-2013	$0		7	$0	$0	$0	$0	$1,026	$4,008	$297	$8,136	$77	$29,564	7
Jun-2013	$0		8	$0	$0	$0	$0	$1,026	$3,110	$297	$7,879	$77	$29,573	8
Jul-2013	$0		9	$0	$0	$0	$0	$1,026	$2,135	$297	$7,621	$77	$29,582	9
Aug-2013	$0		10	$0	$0	$0	$0	$1,026	$1,145	$297	$7,361	$77	$29,591	10
Sep-2013	$0		11	$0	$0	$0	$0	$1,026	$138	$297	$7,100	$77	$29,601	11
Oct-2013	$0		12	$0	$0	$0	$0	$140	$0	$1,183	$5,953	$77	$29,610	12
Nov-2013	$0		13	$0	$0	$0	$0	$0	$0	$1,323	$4,650	$77	$29,620	13
Dec-2013	$0		14	$0	$0	$0	$0	$0	$0	$1,323	$3,350	$77	$29,629	14
Jan-2014	$0		15	$0	$0	$0	$0	$0	$0	$1,323	$2,062	$77	$29,638	15
Feb-2014	$0		16	$0	$0	$0	$0	$0	$0	$1,323	$736	$77	$29,648	16
Mar-2014	$0		17	$0	$0	$0	$0	$0	$0	$743	$0	$657	$29,077	17
Apr-2014	$0		18	$0	$0	$0	$0	$0	$0	$0	$0	$1,400	$27,762	18
May-2014	$0		19	$0	$0	$0	$0	$0	$0	$0	$0	$1,400	$26,443	19
Jun-2014	$0		20	$0	$0	$0	$0	$0	$0	$0	$0	$1,400	$25,120	20
Jul-2014	$0		21	$0	$0	$0	$0	$0	$0	$0	$0	$1,400	$23,793	21
Aug-2014	$0		22	$0	$0	$0	$0	$0	$0	$0	$0	$1,400	$22,463	22
Sep-2014	$0		23	$0	$0	$0	$0	$0	$0	$0	$0	$1,400	$21,128	23
Oct-2014	$0		24	$0	$0	$0	$0	$0	$0	$0	$0	$1,400	$19,790	24
Nov-2014	$0		25	$0	$0	$0	$0	$0	$0	$0	$0	$1,400	$18,448	25
Dec-2014	$0		26	$0	$0	$0	$0	$0	$0	$0	$0	$1,400	$17,102	26
Jan-2015	$0		27	$0	$0	$0	$0	$0	$0	$0	$0	$1,400	$15,751	27
Feb-2015	$0		28	$0	$0	$0	$0	$0	$0	$0	$0	$1,400	$14,397	28
Mar-2015	$0		29	$0	$0	$0	$0	$0	$0	$0	$0	$1,400	$13,039	29
Apr-2015	$0		30	$0	$0	$0	$0	$0	$0	$0	$0	$1,400	$11,677	30
May-2015	$0		31	$0	$0	$0	$0	$0	$0	$0	$0	$1,400	$10,311	31
Jun-2015	$0		32	$0	$0	$0	$0	$0	$0	$0	$0	$1,400	$8,942	32
Jul-2015	$0		33	$0	$0	$0	$0	$0	$0	$0	$0	$1,400	$7,568	33
Aug-2015	$0		34	$0	$0	$0	$0	$0	$0	$0	$0	$1,400	$6,190	34
Sep-2015	$0		35	$0	$0	$0	$0	$0	$0	$0	$0	$1,400	$4,808	35
Oct-2015	$0		36	$0	$0	$0	$0	$0	$0	$0	$0	$1,400	$3,422	36
Nov-2015	$0		37	$0	$0	$0	$0	$0	$0	$0	$0	$1,400	$2,032	37
Dec-2015	$0		38	$0	$0	$0	$0	$0	$0	$0	$0	$1,400	$638	38
Jan-2016	$0		39	$0	$0	$0	$0	$0	$0	$0	$0	$640	$0	39

Questions We Often Get

Should I save or pay down debt?

Many of our clients ask if they should be saving if they're still in debt. The answer is usually yes. Saving is much more fun to do than paying down debt, which means you are more likely to do it. It doesn't mean you take your focus off paying down your debt; it just means that it's okay to save for your goals now. Even starting with a small amount each month will keep your goals alive and get you thinking about how you can achieve them. And for many of us if we waited to start to save until we were out of debt, we might never start. Before you start saving, just make sure you have a clear plan to pay off your debt.

Should I borrow to invest?

With interest rates at historic lows, some investment advisors are encouraging investors to look at the merits of leveraged investing.

Is this a good idea? Maybe, but first look at your reasons for wanting to borrow to invest. Are you hoping to make up the money you lost in the stock market over the past few years? Do you feel like you're just not getting ahead fast enough and want to implement what can sound like a sophisticated investment strategy? Or perhaps you're facing increasing pressure from your investment advisor to put more money into a hot market.

There are conscientious advisors out there who can be of great assistance in advising you about the pluses and minuses of leveraged investing, but you should also take responsibility yourself to make sure this strategy fits with your goals, your personality and your risk tolerance.

Are reward points worthwhile?

Many of our clients love to use their credit card to earn reward points. But should they? These programs are designed to encourage you to use credit for everything from groceries to travel and dining out. Yes, it's great to get the points, but if the ease of using credit cards causes you to overspend (which is so easy to do), you might need to re-think the benefits. Overspending on your credit card by just $50 per month can negate any reward points earned throughout the year, not to mention annual fees of up to $120. If you always pay off your credit cards monthly and you are sticking with your *On Track Money Management System*, reward cards may work for you. If not, best to avoid the temptation.

A Good Credit History Is Important

Using credit wisely is critical to building a solid credit history. Important? Absolutely! Your credit history is what banks and other creditors use to assess how risky it could be to lend you money—and how much interest to charge you. The way you have handled your debts in the past and how much debt you currently have will affect a lender's decision to lend you money and it may affect the amount of interest they charge you. If you need a loan or a mortgage, or you want to renegotiate a loan, a good credit rating is important and will help you negotiate the best terms.

Considering the current economy and subsequent credit crunch, it is not only helpful, but crucial that you find out exactly what information is on your credit report.

In Canada, your credit history is tracked by two major credit tracking companies: Equifax Canada Inc. (equifax.ca) and TransUnion of Canada (transunion.ca). They keep records of where you work, the loans you have, what credit cards you use, and if you have ever filed for bankruptcy.

Your credit history can be connected to other people (past and present). If you co-signed a loan that wasn't paid, this will affect your credit history. If your name is still on a credit card that your ex is using that will also affect your credit. If your children have cell phones under your name and they are ditching their bills, you might pay the price when it comes time to refinance your mortgage.

Have you ever missed, or been late making a credit card payment? Have you ever maxed out your line of credit? Was a long-forgotten bill sent to collections? Has a family member, roommate, ex-spouse, or identify thief left you on the hook for something? All of these things can seriously affect your credit score. Your credit score is a numeric snapshot of your credit risk at a particular point in time. The score is a three-digit number that lenders use to help them make decisions about whether or not to lend you money. A credit score of 700 or above is considered a good rating.

If you have never had credit of any kind, if you are just starting out, or if you have always had credit in your partner's name, you won't have a credit history. Since there is no way for a potential lender to assess the risk associated with lending to you, you might find it very challenging to get a loan if and when you need one. It is a good idea to have some well-managed credit in your name. You don't need five credit cards to have a good credit history. You just need to show that you can manage debt responsibly and pay on time.

A company or individual needs your consent and a legitimate business reason to obtain a copy of your credit report. You can also request a copy of the information yourself. There are various online reports available for a fee. You can also request a free copy by mailing an application to TransUnion or Equifax (see their websites for more details). If the information on your credit report is not accurate or up to date, immediately contact the credit reporting agencies to correct the information.

If you have hiccups in your history, don't panic. Lenders often give you a chance to explain if there were extraordinary circumstances. (Going to the Caribbean for six months and ditching your bills is extraordinarily bad practice but it isn't really what a lender would consider extraordinary circumstances.) You can explain an unpaid bill that was lost in the mail or a temporary period of missed payments immediately following an accident. And if you can demonstrate a marked improvement in your financial dealings post-hiccup, you will be in a much stronger position overall.

Ways to Improve Your Credit Rating

- Pay all of your bills on time. Paying late, or having your account sent to a collection agency will reflect negatively on your credit score.
- Don't run up your balances on your credit limit. Keeping your account balances below 75% of your available credit will help your score.
- Avoid applying for credit unless you really need it. Too many inquiries in a short period of time *might* indicate that you are experiencing financial challenges and looking for credit to make ends meet.
- Contact the credit agencies if you see anything on your credit report that is inaccurate.

When Unconscious Spending Becomes a Problem

We've probably all hit the shops from time to time to give ourselves a little boost. A new outfit or something cool for the house can certainly be a good mood booster. But when does a little 'retail therapy', something innocuous and comforting, become a more serious issue? When does the fun end and the addictive behaviour take over?

Psychologists have been looking at the reasons people deal with depression and anxiety by taking a trip to the mall. Most of the time, they find that shopping is a simple pleasure enjoyed throughout history by people of all cultures, whether at the village market, the great trading bazaars of the Orient, or within the delights of the local mall. In these cases, there is no major reason for guilt or shame or buyer's remorse.

More serious problem shopping, however, has been classified by researchers in Australia as a psychological disorder called oniomania, or compulsive shopping disorder. The clients that we typically deal with would not be considered 'shopaholics' by any means. They do, however have some important spending issues they want or need to deal with.

Most people just spend unconsciously—going out for dinner because they're tired and don't feel like cooking, or treating themselves to a manicure as a reward because they work hard. Maybe they put their vacation on a credit card and hope for the best to pay it off in the next few months. It often boils down to some disorganization, a little laziness, easy access to credit, and no clear goals or priorities.

OUR CLIENT SUSAN was one of those people. What it came down to was that Susan wasn't clear enough on her priorities which led to her overspending. She was in a job she wasn't happy with and spent to alleviate the stress. Shopping was a welcome break from the day-to-day struggles at work.

After much discussion it turned out that Susan wanted to quit her job and start her own consulting business. She knew she could make a good income as a consultant, but felt stuck in her stressful job because she had accumulated so much debt. The thought of quitting and striking out on her own was unfathomable with her debt load.

Once she verbalized her true goal of quitting her job and moving towards consulting, it was clear what she needed to do. She cut up most of her credit cards, went for a walk at lunch instead of heading to the mall and made a plan to be debt-free in 12 months.

As a visual reminder of her goals and priorities, she used a Money Coaches Canada credit card condom for her one remaining credit card. On the front of the credit card condom she wrote down her #1 Goal: "Freedom!" To Susan freedom

meant being free to quit her job when she wanted to, being free to choose who she works with and most of all being free from the unending cycle of debt she was in.

Now when she pulls out her credit card she has an instant reminder of her #1 priority. On the back of the credit card condom there are four questions she asks herself before she spends money on the card:

1. Do I need this right now?
2. Can I afford this?
3. Could I get this cheaper or free elsewhere?
4. Will it move me one step closer to my goal?

Susan now finds it easy to walk past the mall without even considering buying a new blouse or more kitchen gadgets. She has started working with consulting clients part-time to earn more money and to build up her contacts. She recommitted to her job and knows that if she sticks it out for a year she will have the choice and freedom to leave if she is ready to consult full-time.

Where to Turn for Help If Debt is a Serious Problem

With rising costs taking their toll, high consumer debt loads, low savings rates, and poor spending and credit habits, it is quite understandable that declaring bankruptcy sometimes seems like an attractive option. In some cases the stress, anxiety and financial restrictions are simply too much to handle and there is no other reasonable way out.

Every year in Canada more than 100,000 individuals file for personal bankruptcy (or file a "consumer proposal," one of the court-mandated alternatives to bankruptcy). Before you decide, check out your alternatives:

- **Contact your Creditors Directly:** Many creditors will be happy to discuss your debt problems and suggest solutions before things get too far out of hand.
- **Debt Consolidation Loan:** Talk to your bank about packaging all or most of your loans into one more manageable loan.
- **Personal Debt Management Program:** Hire a Money Coach or take a course to get you back on track with your money.
- **Credit Counseling Agencies:** Many not-for-profit agencies can help you re-negotiate your credit card loans and other debts, but you can generally expect to be charged fees. Not all creditors will cooperate with these agencies. Do your due diligence.
- **Consolidation Order, also known as Orderly Payment of Debt:** A court order that lets you pay off your debts over three years and frees you from creditor harassment and wage garnishment. (available only in Alberta, Saskatchewan, Prince Edward Island and Nova Scotia).
- **Proposal(s):** Under the Bankruptcy and Insolvency Act, a trustee or an administrator files a Proposal between you and your creditors to have you pay off only a portion of your debts or extend the repayment time to five years.
- **Debtors Anonymous** (debtorsanonymous.org): This is a good resource for information and support.
- **Bankruptcy** One of the main purposes of bankruptcy legislation is to "afford the opportunity to a person, who is hopelessly burdened with debt, to free himself of the debt and start fresh." While having a new lease on life can sound

appealing, bankruptcy also has serious consequences on both a financial and personal level, but if appropriate it can have you out of debt in nine to 21 months. If you are feeling overwhelmed by your debt load, the first step is to figure out how much debt you have and whether you can realistically pay it off in a reasonable time frame.

WHATEVER your debt picture looks like, don't put off dealing with it and seek help sooner rather than later. Find a qualified professional who understands the emotional as well as financial challenges that debt issues bring to the surface and be done with debt forever.

We have helped most of our clients turn their financial situation around in a few months and more often than not, the stress and anxiety is alleviated at the very first meeting. Just taking that first step towards financial control is enough to break the cycle of frustration and despair. As our client Susan put it: "I wish I had done this sooner. I would be so much further ahead by now."

▸▸10◂◂

||||||||||||||||||||||||||

INVEST
IN YOURSELF

October: This is one of the peculiarly dangerous months
to speculate in stocks in. The others are July,
January, September, April, November, May, March,
June, December, August and February.

MARK TWAIN

AT A RECENT *investing workshop, we asked the group of*
about 40 highly educated, professional women how many
of them fully understood what their money was invested
in. Shockingly, only three people raised their hand which
meant that over 90% of the women in the room had their
money in investments that they couldn't fully explain.

How can this be? In our experience, this is the norm. Most
of our clients come to us with minimal understanding or
interest in the world of money and investing. They feel vulnerable and insecure and, as one of our clients described
it, they feel like 'sitting ducks' when they go into a bank or
visit their financial advisor. They aren't sure what questions to ask and more often than not they don't know what
options are available to them or how to understand and evaluate them. They sign on the dotted line without confidence
or trust.

And if that isn't enough, they're losing confidence in the financial system but they aren't sure what other options they have. And they're concerned that their advisors may have a conflict of interest given that they are selling or managing the investments or financial products that they're recommending.

If you're new to investing and even if you're not, it wouldn't be surprising for you to feel overwhelmed by the sheer number of investment choices available to you. And then there's the lingo to understand.

THE INFORMATION provided here isn't intended to make you an overnight investment expert. It will help you feel more confident in working with your financial planners and investment advisors. And it will give you the big picture so that you can *delegate, not abdicate,* responsibility for the management of your investments. If you'd like to get more involved in managing your own investment portfolio, this is also a good place to start.

In this chapter, we'll give you a primer on investments and information you need to know whether or not you manage your own investments or rely on a financial planner or investment advisor for help. (If you are looking to work with an advisor, refer back to Chapter 5.)

The good news is that once you understand the fundamentals of investing, you'll discover that most investments are really a variation of the basics. Investing doesn't have to be complicated.

Your Goal-Centred Investment Plan

The key to feeling confident about your investments isn't being privy to the latest hot stock tip; it's having a well-thought-out investment plan that supports your ability to make sound decisions, rather than making decisions based on emotions, fear or market fluctuations.

**Your investment plan should reflect
the level of risk you can live with.**

That means striking a balance. You don't want to be pacing the
floor because your money is in stocks you fear will crash. Neither do you want to be pacing the floor because you don't have
enough money for a decent mattress in your golden years!

One of the things that stops people from being comfortable with investing is the risk of losing capital. Of course,
no one wants to lose money on their investments. But there
are other risks that need to be considered as well—such as
the risk of inflation or the risk that you'll outlive your savings. These are risks you face if you don't choose investments
that are appropriate for your goals. And they represent one of
the reasons why you may need to invest at least some of your
money in higher-growth investments.

That is not to say you should take unreasonable or inap-
propriate risk. The key is setting up an investment plan that
is consistent with the level of risk that you're comfortable
with and the time frame you have *before* you need the money
for your goal. As a number of studies have shown, the more
knowledge people have, the more comfortable they are taking the appropriate amount of risk with their investments.

The time frame over which you hold an investment before
it's cashed in or liquidated is known as the investment time
horizon. The longer the time period before you need to use
that money from your investments, the more risk (at least in
theory) you can take on.

In the short run it may feel like investing your money
in higher-growth investments like stocks or stock mutual
funds was a mistake. Or at the very least, you may be quite
uncomfortable if you see the value of your investments go
down. However over the long run, (with long run defined as
seven years or more), higher-growth investments have typically provided higher returns than investments like GICs,
savings accounts or Canada Savings Bonds.

When we say higher-growth investments, it's important to realize that we're not referring to the 'too good to be true' schemes that promise you huge and unrealistic returns from sketchy investments. There is no shortage of stories from the courts and securities regulators about investors who have been burned—many losing virtually all their life savings—by shady investments promising lucrative returns.

Investments and investment plans are not one-size-fits-all
Listen and learn from others, but don't think you can just pick the same investments your sister picks, or your neighbour or your colleague at work; you all may have very different risk profiles and different visions for your life.

The questions you need to ask yourself before investing are:
· What is the money for?
· When do I need the money?
· What investment, or portfolio of investments, would best suit this goal?
· Is my tolerance for risk compatible with this investment or investment portfolio?

The answers to these questions will help you (and your advisor if you choose to work with one) create your **5 Step Goal-Centred Investment Plan.**

STEP 1: Set your investment goals,
STEP 2: Choose your account type
STEP 3: Understand your investment options
STEP 4: Select your investments
STEP 5: Manage and review your investments

STEP 1: Set Your Investment Goals
Your investment decisions must suit the needs of your overall financial plan. And so, as with your financial plan, we

encourage you to design your investment plan goal by goal. There are a lot of investment options out there, but it's easier to make sense of which ones are right for you when you attach your investment decisions to specific goals.

A successful investment plan must begin with your personal and financial goals. Being clear on what you're saving and investing for is essential.

A well-defined investment goal would be something like: "I want to retire in 30 years with an after-tax income of $3,000 a month."

Or it could be: "I want to save $50,000 for the down payment to buy a house in five years."

Remember that investing is simply a tool to help you live the life you want. And unless your financial goals and your investment goals are based on your values and are consistent with your life purpose, you may make money on your investments but you may also find surprisingly little joy in it.

STEP 2: Choose your Account Type

There are two account types to choose from: Accounts that are registered through the Canada Revenue Agency (CRA) are called *registered accounts* and those that aren't are called *non-registered accounts*.

1. Registered accounts include: Registered Savings Plans (RSPS), Registered Retirement Income Funds (RIFS) and Tax Free Savings Accounts (TFSAS).

2. Non-registered accounts are not registered with CRA and are sometimes also referred to as *Open accounts* or *Investment accounts*.

The type of account you chose for the money you have to invest will depend on your goals, personal circumstances, and the amount you are allowed to contribute to registered investments.

Generally speaking RSPS make sense if your goal is retirement and you earn more than $45,000. A TFSA works well if you have maximized your RSPS or if you are in a lower tax bracket. TFSAS can be used for short and long-term goals. RSPS, RIFS and TFSAS have tax advantages that will be discussed in more detail later.

It's important to remember that the investment options outlined in the next section apply to both registered and non-registered accounts.

STEP 3: Understand Your Investment Options
ASSET CLASSES

Most investments fall into three main categories referred to as Asset Classes.

1. Cash

This asset class includes more than just the cash in your pocket or the cash in your chequing account. It refers to investments that tend to be short-term and *liquid* in nature, meaning you can easily access the money without risking a loss in the value of the investment.

Examples include: Savings accounts, Guaranteed Investment Certificates (GICs), Term Deposits (TDS), money market accounts and Canada Savings Bonds.

Cash investments typically have the lowest risk and the lowest potential return.

2. Bonds

A bond is actually an IOU. You agree to loan money to the government, or to a company, and they agree to pay you a specified amount of interest at regular intervals (usually twice a year), and to repay the loan on a specified date. When that date comes up, the bond is said to have *matured*.

At maturity, you are paid the bond's *face value*, which is the amount printed on the bond.

Though bonds are generally quite safe, there are some risks. The company you loan money to could go bankrupt and be unable to pay you back. If interest rates rise, your fixed interest rate could be less than the going rate. And although you can get your money out of a bond by selling it, if your sale is poorly timed, the bond could be valued for less than your investment.

Bond investments generally have medium risk and medium potential return.

3. Stocks, also known as Equities

If you own *stocks*, you actually own a piece of a company. Each piece is called a *share* and you are a *shareholder*.

Stocks could potentially benefit you in two ways:

- Your Stock Value Increases: If the value of your stock goes up over time, your stocks could become worth more than you paid for them. And if at that point you sell your stocks, the difference between your purchase price and your selling price is a type of earnings called *Capital Gains*. Of course, if you don't sell, you can still benefit from seeing a stock value rise. As the value of your asset increases you improve your net worth.
- You Receive Dividends: When an established company makes a profit, it may choose to pay out the profit to its shareholders, rather than invest it back into the company. These payments are called *dividends*. Dividends are often paid quarterly.

Of course, the flip side is that:

- Your Stock Value Decreases: If you have to sell your stocks at a time when they are worth less than what you initially paid, you incur *Capital Losses*, which is a fancy way of saying you've lost some or all of your initial investment.

And just as your net worth improves when the asset gains value, your net worth decreases if the asset loses value.

- Dividends are not Guaranteed: If the company stops making a profit, or if it goes through a change and decides to reinvest the profit in the company, it can stop paying dividends. At that point you could be out of an income stream.

Stock investments generally have higher-risk and higher potential return.

OVER THE 10 years ending December 31, 2016, cash investments earned an average 1.4% return on investment. Bonds averaged 4.8%. And stocks averaged 8.5%.[1] But it's important to keep in mind these are averages and higher-risk investments swing more than lower-risk investments. So although stock investments averaged 8.5%, some years you might see returns in the 20% range and some years in the minus 20% range.

Remember that over the short run the return on higher-risk investments can fluctuate significantly and you might actually find that cash investments in the short run turn out to outperform some of the other investments. However over the long run typically stocks show higher returns than bonds, and bonds show higher returns than cash investments.

As a rule of thumb, cash investments are appropriate if your investment time frame is zero to three years; bonds for three to seven years and stocks for seven-plus years. A combination of two or three asset classes could also be used to diversify a long-term investment plan.

ASSET ALLOCATION

Dividing up your investment dollars between Cash, Bond or Stock investments is called asset allocation.

1 Figures as of December 31, 2016. Numbers have been rounded. Sources: 91 Day TBill Index, FTSE TMX Canada Universe Bond Index, S&P 500 Index.

Asset allocation is a key part of your investment plan because it helps you balance risk and return and maximize the potential for your investments to support your goals and your life. People who don't have an asset allocation plan are really speculating, not investing, and if you want to talk about risk, speculating is risky business.

Studies have shown that it is not the individual investments you choose that determine the overall success of your investment plan, but rather the degree to which you have maximized the benefits of all three asset classes to achieve your goals.

It's unlikely that a single investment will meet all of your investment needs. It's possible that you'll find a single investment for each of your goals, and it's also possible that for a single goal, you'll opt to invest in a combination of investments. The combination of investments you choose is your *investment portfolio*. To ensure you are diversifying your investment portfolio, an appropriate mix of stocks, bonds, mutual funds, real estate and cash can help reduce the overall risk. The specifics will look different for everyone.

Remember, you want to achieve your goals but you also want to achieve well-being, so don't underestimate the importance of including your risk tolerance in your plans.

Sample Asset Allocation Plan

RENA PLANS to retire in 30 years. She has $30,000 already saved in her RSP, but she has just been moving her money from one GIC to another because she didn't understand her investment options and was afraid of losing her money in higher-risk investments. She also wants to invest $200 every month.

After educating herself more on the benefits of investing for the long-term Rena is ready to invest to her best advantage. She has thought it through and although retirement is a long-term goal, she's only starting to build her understanding and confidence with the market. She says she has a medium risk tolerance but wants her RSP to grow so she can reach her retirement goals.

A possible asset allocation for her scenario could be:
10% Cash
30% Bonds
60% Stocks

How did Rena come up with this mix for her asset allocation? Rena doesn't need much in the way of cash investments for this goal because retirement is a long way away, and she now knows that she is comfortable with medium-risk investments. Bonds are a good medium-risk investment but they don't give her the growth she could get in equities. Since Rena wants some growth and has a long time horizon, she is comfortable investing 60% in equities to maximize her investment's growth potential, while at the same time respecting her medium risk tolerance by investing the rest in cash and bonds.

Rena's asset allocation strategy could be applied equally to the money she has already saved, and to the money she plans to invest each month. Here's how it would look:

ASSET ALLOCATION	CURRENT INVESTMENTS	MONTHLY SAVINGS
10% Cash	$3,000	$20
30% Bonds	$9,000	$60
60% Stocks	$18,000	$120
TOTAL	$30,000	$200

How to Figure Out Your Personal Asset Allocation Plan

For each of your investment goals you are going decide: "Which investments are right for me?"

You will answer all the central investing questions and create a plan of action for *each of your goals.*

For each goal you need to answer the following questions:

When will I need the money for my goal?
☐ 1–3 years
☐ 4–7 years
☐ 7 years or more

What is my risk tolerance for this goal?
☐ Low
☐ Medium
☐ High

How comfortable do you feel with the ups and downs of the investing world? Consider your feelings about risk for each of your goals as your tolerance for risk may be lower or higher depending on the goal in question. You might feel very comfortable taking some risk for your retirement, but not for your children's education fund.

What am I looking for?
☐ Safety
☐ Income
☐ Growth

For instance, if you are retired you may find that you need *income* from your investments. Or your objective might be having your investment *grow* as much as it possibly can. Sometimes it's going to be a mix of each of these objectives, but just rank them in order of priority. If the category doesn't apply, mark it 'not applicable.'

The next step is to decide on your asset allocation for each investment goal. Your unique asset allocation is dependent on the answers to the above questions for each goal.

If, for instance, you're saving for retirement that is 10 years away and you're comfortable with the ups and downs of the investment markets, your asset allocation could be:

10% Cash

20% Bonds

70% Stocks

If, on the other hand, your goal was to save for a house down payment that you need in two years, your investment time frame is short so you would want to keep your money safe and very liquid. Your asset allocation would be:

100% Cash

0% Bonds

0% Stocks

CONSIDER LACEY and her sisters, who are saving up to host their parents' 40th wedding anniversary. The sisters are spread out all over Canada so it will be a big surprise to have the whole family together.

They need enough money to fly all four sisters and their families to Regina, host a dinner reception for 40 people, and pay for hotel rooms and little extras. And they want to build up a kitty so that they can promise their parents that they'll all be together again for their 50th.

Their goal is to have $12,000 within 12 months for the 40th anniversary party, and save another $8,000 over 10 years.

Here's what they decided: All four sisters contribute $250 a month to savings accounts. In 12 months, they will have saved enough to pay for the 40th anniversary.

Also they pooled their money and bought $4,000 of stock mutual funds, which they hope will average a 7% return. At that rate, they could double their investment in 10 years.

By putting 60% of their investment money into safer investments (e.g. high-interest savings accounts), they guarantee they'll have money for the short-term part of their goal.

And by putting 40% of their money into stock mutual funds, they are letting the market pay for half of the next celebration. Although they know there are no guarantees with stock mutual funds, they're comfortable taking the risk for this longer-term goal.

Bear in mind that creating an asset allocation plan is not an exact science and different advisors may interpret the criteria a little differently. The main take-away is that the logic behind creating an asset allocation plan should consider the principles of time frame and risk tolerance and it should pass your common sense test.

STEP 4: Select Your Investments

The next step is to choose the specific investments that match your asset allocation plan. Will you invest in individual securities like stocks or bonds, or will you invest in mutual funds, exchange-traded funds (ETFs) or index funds or a mix of several of these options?

MUTUAL FUNDS

Mutual funds are an easy way to invest in any or all of the asset classes. Instead of buying a single bond or stock, you pool your money with a lot of other investors to buy *units*, or shares of a mutual fund.

Mutual funds are managed by professional money managers employed by mutual fund companies. They use the pool of investor money to buy (and sell) cash, bonds and stocks on a massive scale, much larger than any average investor. Then they group investments together to achieve strategic investment objectives.

Some mutual funds will include only assets from a particular asset classification. If a mutual fund is made up of cash assets, it would be considered a lower-risk fund. A mutual fund that is comprised of a variety of stocks would fall into a higher-risk category.

Mutual funds that hold a mix of cash, bonds, and stocks are generally called *Balanced Funds*.

The value of a mutual fund is affected by the value of all the individual investments in the fund. So if your mutual fund is made up of 12 stocks, and 10 go up, while two go down, in theory, you will enjoy a value increase and you won't feel the burn of those two individual dips. Generally, balanced funds take this a step further because they combine lower-risk investments with higher-risk investments, thus reducing the overall risk of the investment.

Mutual funds have many advantages for the average investor, including:

Affordability
Most mutual fund companies have low minimum investment amounts; you can start investing with as little as $25 per month.

Monthly Contributions
Mutual funds are designed for you to be able to make monthly contributions. The market changes every day. Some people wait to invest because they think they have to time their purchase strategically. But if you automatically invest a constant amount each month, say $50, the price fluctuations mean that some months you will buy more units than others with the same amount of cash. Over time, you average out the ups and the downs, so market timing isn't an issue. This is called '*Dollar Cost Averaging*.'

Diversification
Diversification means that you don't have all your eggs in one basket. The idea behind the mutual fund is that by grouping investments together in a single fund, the mutual fund company helps protect its investors from the value swings of any single investment. This spreads out your risk. And if you

invest in more than one type of mutual fund, you spread the risk even further.

Expertise

Mutual funds are managed by professional money managers who have the experience, do the research and watch the trends.

Disclosure

Stringent regulations outline how mutual funds must be set up and managed, and how investors are informed. Before you invest you will be given a document called a *prospectus,* which, amongst other things, itemizes fees and lists the investments in the mutual fund.

Flexibility

You can easily buy and sell your units in a mutual fund. You aren't locked in.

International investments

It can be hard for the average investor to buy stocks and bonds outside of Canada (with the exception of the US). Mutual funds make it easy, and again, a knowledgeable professional is monitoring the international markets for you.

Some people mistakenly assume that mutual funds are higher-risk investments, but that isn't necessarily the case. The risk associated with any mutual fund is determined by the investments that are held within each mutual fund. This means that some mutual funds can be low-risk (eg. money market mutual funds) and some can be higher-risk (eg. stock mutual funds).

You can be involved in choosing the type of mutual funds that you want by doing your own research or you can have an investment advisor, broker or financial planner help you decide which mutual funds to buy.

It's up to the mutual fund manager to decide when it is a good time to buy certain stocks or bonds and when it is a good time to sell them. For this service, of course, there's going to be a cost.

MUTUAL FUND FEES

Chances are you own or have owned a mutual fund at some time. But do you know how much you are paying for your funds? Because you don't usually see the fees you are paying on your statement, it's easy to ignore the issue of investment fees.

New regulations requiring financial institutions to provide fee and rate of return information will help Canadian investors better understand their costs and how well their mutual funds are performing. Not all fees are disclosed on the new reports so be sure to ask your advisor for clarification.

Are we getting our money's worth? Pretty hard to tell unless you understand some of the industry lingo and what goes into the mutual fund fee calculation.

Take *management fees* and *management expense ratios*. It's a common mistake for investors to use the terms interchangeably, but they are definitely not the same.

Management fees represent the payment to the mutual fund managers for selecting the investments to include in the fund. The management fee may also include fees paid to the advisor's firm that sold the fund and is meant to cover the cost of advice to the client.

Management fees are only one component of the overall fees you are charged. The number that you should really be interested in is the *management expense ratio,* or MER.

The MER includes the management fees plus other indirect costs such as: fund administration charges, legal, audit, custodian fees and transfer agent fees, advertising and marketing expenses and taxes.

And just how much of a difference is there between the two charges? Let's look at an example. ABC Mutual Fund Company offers a Canadian stock mutual fund with a management fee of 2%. After adding in all the other charges, the MER comes out at 2.5%.

So where does the MER show up in your fund? It isn't easy to see because MERS typically aren't listed on your investment statements and the published rate of return (what you actually earn from the fund) is calculated *after* including these fees.

LET'S SAY you own ABC Canadian Stock fund and the published rate of return as of the end of the year is 5.5%. This means that from January 1 to December 31 of that year, the value of the stocks in your fund increased by 8% before the MER of 2.5% was applied. Your return after fees is calculated as 8% less 2.5%, which equals 5.5%. If you had invested $5,000 in ABC Canadian Stock fund on January 1, your investment would be worth $5,275 on December 31 of that year.

MER information is published in the prospectus that you are given when you buy a mutual fund and can also be found on mutual fund information websites like globefund.com and morningstar.ca or by asking your advisor.

When comparing MERS from one fund to another make sure that you are comparing apples to apples. Typically management expenses ratios are highest for the specialty stock mutual funds and lowest for money market funds. Bond and balanced funds fall somewhere in the middle. Don't try to compare the MER from one fund to another if the underlying investments are from different asset classes.

Because the MER can include commissions and trailer fees paid to financial planners and investment advisors for providing service and advice to investors, these funds (often referred to as 'load' mutual funds) may have higher MERs than some bank funds or 'factory direct' mutual funds. Some of the better known 'load' mutual funds companies like Mackenzie, Fidelity, CI and Templeton are funds offered through financial planners and investment advisors.

Factory direct funds like those offered by Phillips Hager and North, Leith Wheeler, Mawer, or Steadyhand to name a few, often have lower MERs because they sell their funds directly to the investor through their own in-house advisors.

Load mutual funds purchased through your financial advisor may also have a redemption charge so be sure to talk to your advisor to ensure you understand what fees you are paying and if there are any charges when you sell your funds.

SHOULD YOU always go for the lowest fee funds? Of course it's better to keep more in your pocket, but you also have to weigh the value of advice. If your advisor is giving you great service and top-notch financial planning and investment advice, then as long as you know what you're paying for and see value, don't fix what isn't broken. If not, it might be time to explore some of the lower expense investment options.

MUTUAL FUNDS VERSUS EXCHANGE-TRADED FUNDS (ETFS)

For most Canadians, mutual funds are a mainstay of their investment portfolio. Many investors, however are angry and frustrated with the high fees they're being charged and with mutual funds that barely outperform the market—if they do that. (Studies are showing that 70-80% do not outperform.) The big question we are often asked is whether to switch out of mutual funds into exchange-traded funds.

In a couple of important respects ETFs are similar to mutual funds: they are packages of investments bundled by a financial institution for sale to the investor, and they're designed to diversify risk and opportunity. The essential distinction of ETFs is that they are a basket of investments tied to a specific 'index,' such as the S&P/TSX composite index, Dow Jones Industrial Average or the S&P 500. Your ETF investment therefore mirrors the fortunes of whatever index your ETF fund is tied to. If it's tied to the S&P/TSX, largely comprised of bank and commodity stocks, and it does well, then you do well. If not...well, you get the picture.

HERE ARE some things to consider in making your decision on whether to purchase mutual funds or ETFs:

Lower fees are certainly a good reason to consider an indexing strategy. Fees for indexing typically range between 0.5% and 1.0%—as opposed to costs of up to 3.0% for equity mutual funds.

ETF fees are lower for three primary reasons. First, they do not require the same level of market research that mutual funds do, because they simply track an index instead of a professional manager deciding on the merits and demerits of a bundle of stocks. Second, they are mainly sold through discount brokerage firms and this helps to keep costs down. Third, with ETFs you get little or nothing in the way of advice or service.

Lower fees are not everything, however. One of the main downsides to ETFs is that you are largely on your own to research, evaluate, and buy and sell them. There are now hundreds of ETFs to choose from and you have to ask yourself if you're really willing to do the background investigative work.

One reason to invest in a mutual fund portfolio is the advice that you get—or should get—when investing this way. Yes you pay more, but a good advisor will consider such things as your risk tolerance, net worth, your retirement plans, and the rest of your portfolio mix, to better advise you on the funds that are best suited to you at the various stages of your financial life.

Whatever route you decide to go—ETFs, traditional or lower cost ('factory direct') mutual funds—you will be best served if you keep your investment decisions in line with your overall financial objectives and the time and energy you want to devote to your investments.

HOW MUCH CASH SHOULD YOU HOLD?

Risk-averse Canadians are sitting on a lot of cash these days and some experts are warning that the country's cash holdings are now so large that they could jeopardize Canada's economic recovery. The other problem is that we're not getting a good return on cash holdings. So should we hold cash or not?

Rates of return for so-called high-interest savings accounts currently run between 0.5% and 1%, and five-year GICs have been returning 3.5% or less for some time, often closer to 2%. And of course, over the long run, cash investments haven't done as well as bonds or stock investments. But still, cash can be an important component of your investment plan.

There's much more to investment planning than just getting the best rate of return. Sure inflation is an important consideration. So too, is having enough money to meet future expenses and goals. BUT—if your investments are ultimately designed to help you enjoy your life, then you need to consider the emotional as well as the dollars and cents implications of financial security. Being stressed about money doesn't make for good investment decisions or a happy life.

We know firsthand the value to clients of being more educated about how money and investments work—greater understanding of money usually leads to better financial decisions and less worry. But we also know that graphs, charts, and financial calculations can only go so far to relieve the anxiety caused by market fluctuations.

So what do these concerns mean to your portfolio?

Let's start with a simple and obvious fact. We're human. Sometimes we make irrational decisions based on emotions— sometimes fear, sometimes greed, sometimes wishful thinking. Even though we know we should keep our emotions from dictating our investment decisions, it is unlikely that our species is going to change this type of instinctual behaviour anytime soon.

So you need to make investment decisions that suit all of your needs—including the very human need and desire for security. This means that cash investments should always be an integral part of your portfolio. The amount of cash you should hold is largely dependent on two factors. First is your tolerance for risk. The second factor is your need for cash in the near future.

For instance, if you don't want to take any market risk at all, then your choices are pretty much limited to a 100% cash or government bond portfolio. (If you take this approach, you should run the precise numbers to be sure that you'll have enough to cover your long-term needs after tax and after inflation.)

And even if you can accept a high level of risk in your overall portfolio, but need to use some of your funds in the next two to three years, your best bet is to hold the amount you will need in cash or near-cash investments.

How does this work?

Let's say you want to buy a house in two years but first have to save for the down payment. Your existing savings and any new money you save should be held in cash investments so you can be sure that the money is there when you need it— regardless of what happens in the markets.

Or if you're at retirement age and you need $3,000 a month ($36,000 annually) to fund your lifestyle, then keep a reserve of about $108,000 in cash to fund the next three years. This will give you the emotional upside of knowing that you have cash in the bank and you will be financially okay for the next few years.

By holding cash for your two to three year short term needs, you will be more comfortable with your other higher-risk investments that you need for growth. Then even when the markets fluctuate wildly, it will be easier for you to resist the temptation to react emotionally because you know that some of your portfolio is protected. It may not sound like an exciting strategy but a good night's sleep sure makes sense to us.

HOW INVESTMENTS ARE TAXED

When making your investment decisions, it is wise to consider the various tax implications—both positive and negative.

As always, first remember that your investments should reflect your goals and values, your time frame and your risk tolerance. Tax advantages can change with the government, investment decisions should change with your life.

That said, here are some important guidelines on how investments are taxed for you to keep in mind:

Registered Investments (RSPS & RIFS)— You get a tax deduction when you contribute to your RSP and your earnings grow tax free. RSPs are not taxed until you remove money from your registered investment. You will then be taxed at the rate applicable on your income at withdrawal, which is usually at a lower rate at retirement than when you were working.

Non-Registered Investments—Interest: Interest on non-registered investments is fully taxable at your applicable tax rate. If you have money in non-registered investments, it is important to note that safer investments tend to be taxed more heavily.

If you earn 3% a year in interest on a $10,000 GIC, you will have earned $300. If your marginal tax rate is 30%, you will owe $90 of your earnings in taxes and you will be left with $210.

Non-Registered Investments—Dividends: Dividend income from non-registered investments in Canadian companies qualifies for the dividend tax credit. This is an incentive for Canadians to invest in Canadian companies.

Non-Registered Investments—Capital Gains: Capital gains are taxable on non-registered investments at your applicable tax rate—but only on 50% of your realized capital gains. Investments, such as stocks, bonds and certain types of mutual funds typically *realize* capital gains (or capital losses) in the year you sell. If your stock value goes up but you don't sell, the gain is not *realized* yet, and therefore not taxed.

If you bought a stock for $1,000 and it grew to be worth $1,400 on the day you sell it, you would realize a gain of $400. But since only 50% of that is taxed, you only have to add $200 to your taxable income. If your marginal rate is 30%, you would pay only $60 in tax and you would get to keep $340.

If you hold mutual funds (even if you don't sell them) at tax time you might get a T3 slip reporting a capital gain. This is because the fund manager has sold investments within the fund that has a realized capital gain. When you sell your mutual fund, you will need to have records of the 'adjusted cost base' of your fund to report your capital gain or loss on your tax return. You can get this information from your mutual fund company or investment advisor.

TAX-FREE SAVINGS ACCOUNTS (TFSAS)
In 2009, the federal government introduced a new incentive for Canadians to save and invest. When you save or

invest money in a TFSA, the income accumulated will not be taxed. To give you a better understanding of this new kind of account, we have compiled a list of common questions about the TFSA.

Who can contribute to a TFSA?

Any Canadian over the age of 18 who files a tax return is eligible to contribute to a TFSA.

Where can I set up a TFSA?

All banks, credit unions and financial institutions offer TFSAS.

What types of investments can I hold in my TFSA?

You can hold any type of RSP-eligible investment including publicly traded stocks, bonds, mutual funds, ETFs and cash deposits.

How much can I contribute to a TFSA?

With the launch of the TFSA in 2009 the annual contribution was set at $5,000 per year. The annual contribution limit is to be indexed to inflation in $500 increments. In 2013, the contribution limit was increased to $5,500. Any unused contributions will add to your next year's contribution room. Your unused contribution room carries over indefinitely. For example, if you had not contributed to a TFSA since the program launched in 2009, you would have $52,000 of available room in 2017. This applies even if you haven't opened an account. (Note: contribution limit was increased to $10,000 in 2015 only.)

Are contributions to a TFSA tax-deductible?

Unlike RSPs, contributions to TFSAs are not tax-deductible.

Who keeps track of my contribution room?

The Canada Revenue Agency (CRA) will track your TFSA room

just as they do your RSP contribution room. Inquire by registering for My Account at cra.gc.ca/myaccount or by calling the CRA.

What are the Advantages of a TFSA?

- Investment income (such as interest, dividends and capital gains) earned in your TFSA will not be taxed. Your savings and investments grow tax-free.
- Withdrawals from a TFSA do not affect government benefits that are income tested such as Old Age Security (OAS), Guaranteed Income Supplements (GIS) or GST/HST credits.
- You can withdraw money from your account at any time.

What should I use a TFSA for?

A TFSA can provide additional savings for retirement and can also be used for shorter-term goals such as saving for a trip, emergency fund, wedding or to buy a home.

When can I withdraw funds from my TFSA?

You can withdraw funds from your TFSA at any time and you will not pay tax on the income or withdrawal amount. In addition, the amount withdrawn from your account will be added to your contribution room for the coming year. This means you can reinvest the money that you withdraw at a later date.

A Note On Real Estate

Real Estate is actually an asset class all its own. There are a few ways you can invest in real estate:

Primary Residence you can own your own home

Rental Property you can buy a property and rent it out

Recreational Property you can buy a cottage, hobby farm or time-share

Real Estate Investment Trust (REIT) you can buy shares in a

real estate company that holds income-producing properties.

Owning your home has significant long-term advantages but you still need to look carefully at how an investment in real estate impacts your overall plan. Property values tend to cycle through ups and downs and they are very dependent on the overall economy of the region.

It is important that you give real estate careful consideration and not assume it is a "must have" investment.

Most people buy homes to live in; the investment advantages are a bonus. Whether you are looking at real estate for personal use, or strictly as an investment, be sure to think long-term and ask yourself:

- Is this investment consistent with my goals?
- Can I maintain or increase the value of the investment (Maintenance, decor, landscaping)?
- Can I afford the monthly payments, and maintenance, and live the life I want?
- Do I have an emergency fund for unexpected maintenance?
- Am I prepared to be someone's landlord (If you are thinking of renting out the property)?

Consider the sheer size of the investment—it is a large amount of money to be allocated to a single investment. And consider the fact that you can't really access the money in the investment until you sell. By comparison, if you had the same amount of money invested in mutual funds, and you needed to withdraw 10% of it for any reason, you could sell 10% of your mutual funds. You can't sell your bathroom. However home ownership may be a strong personal goal for you and that can be worth more than any potential investment advantage.

A Special Note For First Time Home Buyers
If you are a first time buyer, and you have RSPs, you may

be eligible to use the Home Buyers' Plan to withdraw up to $25,000 from your RSP to buy your first home. If you take advantage of this opportunity, you have to repay the total amount withdrawn from your RSP within 15 years and your minimum annual repayment is $1/15$ of the total. Say you withdrew the full $25,000, your minimum repayment would be $1,667 per year, or $139 per month. If you are unable to repay it, the annual repayment amount will be added to your taxable income for the year.

STEP 5: Manage and Review Your Investments

And finally, the last step in Your Goal-Centred Investment Plan is to manage and review your investments. No matter what investments you choose, or who is managing your investments, you need to review your portfolio at least once a year. If you are working with an advisor, make sure you ask for rate of return information and review how this compares to the appropriate market benchmarks. Look at one, three, five and 10 year rate of return figures so you know how well your investments are really doing.

But a word of caution: If the markets aren't doing well it may be hard to resist the temptation to do something in order to relieve the anxiety that goes along with a portfolio drop. The problem is this is often exactly the wrong thing to do.

Here's what usually happens: The worst performing funds are sold, then recent strong performers are recommended and chosen as replacement funds. Let's face it—it's pretty hard to convince a client to move into a fund that has shown negative returns recently.

Unless the portfolio was badly planned up front or there are truly valid reasons for moving out of the 'dog' fund, switching funds usually amounts to 'selling low' and 'buying high.' Emotionally, both client and advisor are temporarily satisfied by taking action, but this is clearly not a good strategy for making money long-term.

Dalbar Inc., a Boston consulting group, found that the average mutual fund investor usually gets a much lower return on their investment than the performance reported by the fund itself. Why? Because of switches made in a chase for performance.

A better approach is to do your homework in advance of investing, come up with a game plan and then stick to it. Having too many options makes it difficult even for professionals to make comparisons, track performance and resist making fund switches. Spend the time up front to create a solid, disciplined plan then forget about it. Don't be compelled to keep tinkering and making changes unless there is a very good reason to do so.

REBALANCING

When reviewing your investments annually, you may need to adjust your portfolio if it has deviated from your desired asset allocation. Let's say your asset allocation plan is as follows:

10% Cash
30% Bonds
60% Stocks

You are comfortable that this plan is still in line with your goals and risk tolerance.

At annual review time you realize that your asset allocation has changed. After 12 months in the market your portfolio now looks like this:

10% Cash
20% Bonds
70% Stocks

One reason this could happen is that the value of the stock portion of your portfolio rose faster than the value of the bond portion. While it is nice to see the value of your stocks go up, you are now are holding a higher percentage in stocks than originally planned and you have increased the level of risk in your portfolio.

To bring your portfolio back in line with your asset allocation plan, you will need to sell stocks and buy bonds to *rebalance* the investments back to the desired original asset allocation.

If you are working with an advisor, an annual review and rebalancing should be part of the service they offer to you.

CHANGE YOUR INVESTMENTS WHEN YOUR LIFE CHANGES, NOT WHEN THE MARKET DOES.

You may also need to adjust your portfolio if you experience:
- a change in your life circumstances (e.g. you get married, have kids, retire)
- a change in your goals
- a change in your risk tolerance
- a change in the time horizon for your goals
- aging. Younger people tend to hold more stocks or stock mutual funds, because they have time to ride out the dips. You may shift to a more cautious approach as you near retirement. After retirement, you will want to focus more on income investments because they will provide for your cash flow needs.

You now have the basic framework to start investing with confidence. Be sure to take a life-long approach to both investing and learning about investing, but start today. Make a phone call or start researching online. Go for it. Make your money work for you, and use it to live your best life.

▸▸11◂◂

||||||||||||||||||||||||||

DON'T GIVE UP
ON RETIREMENT YET

The question isn't at what age
I want to retire, it's at what income.
GEORGE FOREMAN

THINK RETIREMENT IS out of your grasp? The recent economic downturn and the consequent impact on investments have caused many people to worry about their retirement and to re-think their options. The financial news these days can certainly be disheartening, but things might not be as bad as you think. Do you really know where you stand?

The fact is about one-third of Canadians with less than five years to retirement don't have a retirement plan. If you are one of those who hasn't mapped out a plan yet you might be worrying and putting off that next stage of life for nothing.

OUR CLIENT MARY came to us worried that she might never be able to retire and would have to continue to work at a job she didn't like for the long haul. She had thought of having a retirement plan done sooner but was so afraid of what she might find out that she keep putting it off. We worked with Mary to figure out what her lifestyle needs would be in retirement and after crunching the numbers it turned out she had more than enough to retire comfortably immediately. In fact, she could have retired securely several years earlier.

But for most of us, it's challenging to think about retirement and to balance that with the demands on our money today. There's also the question of how much is enough for retirement. We read and hear varying reports in the media and from financial advisors about how much is enough—we worry if we don't have $2 million set aside for retirement, our retirement outlook is bleak.

There is also the ongoing debate over the sustainability of the Canada Pension Plan (CPP) and whether it will, along with Old Age Security (OAS), meet the needs of future Canadian retirees.

Company pension plans aren't filling the gap. Close to four in 10 Canadians are covered by a company pension but even those plans are moving away from guaranteed benefits in the face of increasing economic pressure.

To fill the savings gap, the federal government is aiming to make the CPP a more significant component of Canadians' retirement income with increased benefits funded by higher contributions from employers and employees.

RETIREMENT, or financial independence, ranks as one of people's top financial goals. Despite that, in the face of so many immediate financial pressures, it's easy to avoid thinking about the future. There is a hotbed of emotion that surrounds the question of retirement planning which stops us from even wanting to engage in this conversation and to take proactive steps towards financial independence.

Avoiding the issue though can increase your anxiety over your retirement prospects. What contributes most to the worry is not having enough information about your own personal circumstances: what you need to do and what you can control as far as your retirement is concerned.

When you plan, you can work through different life and

financial scenarios to see where you stand in the future. If you fail to plan, you run a significant risk of ending up with an outcome that you don't like and you never expected. By then it's too late to go back and change the decisions you made along the way.

You may think you're too young to be thinking about retirement or you've waited too long to plan for retirement, but it's never too soon or too late to give yourself choices.

The 5 Biggest Retirement Mistakes You Don't Want to Make

Here are the five biggest retirement mistakes that people make. You'll want to do your best to avoid them:

1. Avoiding the Conversation—That conversation could be with yourself. It could be with a spouse or it could be with an advisor. Having a conversation about retirement helps to bring some clarity to what your goals are. If the conversation is with your spouse or partner, it will give you a sense of whether or not your spouse is on the same page or if they have different ideas about retirement. It doesn't mean you have to have exactly the same vision, but it's very, very useful to have an idea of what direction each of you wants to go.

2. Not being clear about what you want—It's very hard in our day-to-day frenzy of activities to take that step back and say, "Hey, what do I want now and what do I want in the future?" Clarity provides direction and motivation to make good decisions along the way.

3. Being afraid to look at the numbers—Yes, it's a little scary to shed light on what your true situation is, but it's also liberating. When you actually know what your circumstances are, you can figure out what you need to do and then it's easier to take action.

4. Not having control over your expenses—The most important thing you can do to have a healthy financial life now and in the future is to have control over your expenses. It's not easy in light of all the competing demands for your money but learning to live within your means is critical for a comfortable retirement.

5. Carrying debt into retirement—It may not be avoidable, but carrying debt into retirement really limits your flexibility in the future. Aim to be debt-free before you retire.

Your 4 Step Retirement Plan

Creating a retirement plan is a step by step process that will help you answer these questions:

1. What does retirement mean to me and what are my retirement goals?
2. How much money will I need in retirement?
3. Where will my income come from?
4. How much do I have to save now, to have enough in retirement?

STEP 1: What does retirement mean to me?

Just as it was important to dream and set goals for your current life, it's important to do the same for your retirement so that you can build a financial plan accordingly.

Imagine what retirement will look like for you. It's different for everyone, so don't assume that you have to retire at 65 and take cruise ship holidays. Retirement might be the day you trade everything in to buy a pub and guest house in a quaint Irish village. Maybe you will transition from working to volunteering for a cause you have always wanted to support. Maybe you'll finally be able to go back to school.

Start with your dreams about retirement.

IF MONEY WASN'T AN ISSUE, WHAT WOULD YOU DO?

What is your vision of retirement? Will you transition slowly or make a clean break from work? Will you stay in your current home or find a well maintained condo? Will you travel? Will your family be close by? Will you work part-time? Will you volunteer? Will you ski or golf more?

What future do you see?

_____

Where would you live?

_____

What would you be doing?

_____

Who would you be doing it with?

_____

Would you work? How much would you work?

_____

What brings you joy?

_____

What contributions would you make?

_____

What legacy would you leave?

_____

How prepared are you (emotionally, physically, financially) for retirement?

_____

Now set clear, attainable and true retirement goals, and then prioritize them. Write down the goal, the time frame for achieving the goal and an estimated cost. Don't worry about inflation, just write your estimations in today's dollars.

MY RETIREMENT GOALS

EXAMPLES:

1. Retire in 10 years with an after-tax income of $30,000 to cover expenses
2. Pay off the mortgage within 10 years—$130,000
3. Start a home business within five years to bring in extra cash during retirement—start-up costs $10,000

MY RETIREMENT GOALS	COST/VALUE	TIME FRAME
1.		
2.		
3.		
4.		
5.		

STEP 2: How much money will I need to live on in retirement?
The next step is to figure out how much money you will need. There is no magic number. Just as visions are unique, the amount you need for retirement is unique.

Think about how much you will be spending monthly or annually when you reach retirement. The easiest way to estimate your retirement spending is to start with what you are spending right now and then think about what might change in retirement.

- Will you still have a mortgage or other debt?
- Will your children be grown and independent? Will you have to travel to see them?
- Do you or your spouse have health issues that could be a financial burden?
- Do you have travel plans, or dreams that you want to realize in retirement?
- Do you think you will want to stay in your current home? Will you need to hire help?

Go back to your *Spending and Savings Plan* in Chapter 7 to see what you are spending today and then estimate what you think you will need in retirement.

Fill in the *Retirement Lifestyle Expenses* worksheet on the next page, and don't worry about inflation. Just fill it in using today's dollars.

RETIREMENT LIFESTYLE EXPENSES

EXPENSES:

MAIN CHEQUING - Monthly Fixed Costs	Monthly	Annual
Rent / Mortgage		
Condo/Strata Fees		
Property Insurance (if paid monthly)		
Property Taxes (if paid monthly)		
Gas or Oil (for heating)		
Hydro		
Phone		
Cable		
Internet		
Cell Phone(s)		
House Alarm		
Life Insurance Premiums		
Health Insurance Premiums		
Vehicle Payments		
Savings		
Bank Fees		
Vehicle Insurance (if paid monthly)		
Charitable Donation		
Clubs or Gym Membership (if paid monthly)		
Credit Card #1 Pymt		
Credit Card #2 Pymt		
Personal Loan / Student Loan Payment		
Line of Credit Payment		
Other		
Total Monthly Fixed Costs		

MONTHLY SPENDING - Chequing #2	Monthly	Annual
Groceries & Cleaning Supplies		
Pet Food and Treats		
Pharmacy, Toiletries		
Gas for Vehicle		
Taxis / Bus/ Parking		
Snacks and Lunches		
Entertainment - Dining out, Movies, etc.		
Alcohol - (beer/wine) and/or Cigarettes		
Other		
Total Monthly Spending		

SAVINGS ACCOUNTS - Lump Sum and Annual Expenses	Monthly	Annual
Fixed Annual & Lump Sum Expenses		
Property Taxes (if paid annually)		
Vehicle Insurance (if paid annually)		
Property Insurance (if paid annually)		
Clubs & Memberships (if paid annually)		
Magazine Subscriptions		
Costco Membership/Credit Card Annual Fees		
Professional / Accounting Fees		
Variable Annual & Lump Sum Expenses		
Home Repairs, Furniture and Household Items		
Vehicle Repairs and Maintenance		
Medical, Dental, Glasses, Contacts		
Personal Care (hair care, cosmetics, dry cleaning)		
Clothing, Shoes, Outerwear		
Gifts and Donations		
Vet Bills		
Travel, Vacations and Family Fun		
Self-Improvement & Hobbies		
Computer/Electronics		
Other		
Total Lump Sum and Annual Expenses		
TOTAL CASH NEEDS		

Remember to include the costs associated with your retirement lifestyle and costs associates with aging.

STEP 3: Where will my income come from?

The next step is to look at your potential sources of retirement income.

EMPLOYER PENSIONS

There are two kinds of employer pension plans.

1. Defined Benefit Plan

Your employer contributes to a group pension that is professionally managed. Depending on your plan you may be required to contribute as well. This provides you with a guaranteed monthly income at retirement, which is based on your employment income and years of service. Defined benefit pensions may or may not be indexed with inflation.

This income is guaranteed for the rest of your life, and some or all of your benefit may be guaranteed for your spouse after your death. In this way, the employer takes responsibility for having enough money to pay employees a defined amount.

ROB IS 65 and has worked as a teacher with the Huntington School Board for 30 years. He is retiring this year and will receive a defined benefit pension of $3,000/month for the rest of his life. His pension is indexed to inflation which means that the amount he receives will go up by the inflation factor and timing as prescribed by his plan. Because Rob opted for the 60% survivor benefit option, if he dies, his wife Bonnie will receive 60% of Rob's pension for the rest of her life.

2. Defined Contribution Plan

Your employer makes a specific contribution to your retirement plan each month or each year. Depending on your plan you may be required to contribute as well. The accumulated savings is yours at retirement. There are no guarantees on monthly payouts at retirement, or that the savings will last your lifetime.

The employee assumes the risk that the money is well invested. The success of the plan depends on how much you and your employer contribute, how well the investments do and how carefully you draw down the funds at retirement.

IRENE IS 45 and works for Wellington Electric Inc. Both she and her employer contribute 5% of her salary to her defined contribution plan. It is up to Irene to choose how she wants this money invested from the options that the company provides to her. She doesn't plan to retire for 20 years, has medium risk tolerance and is looking for the investments in her pension plan to grow. She decided on the Balanced Growth investment option.

Currently Irene has $100,000 in her defined contribution pension plan. If her pension grows to $300,000 by retirement, this is the amount she will be entitled to when she stops working. There are no guarantees—it will be up to Irene to withdraw the money appropriately to make her pension savings last her lifetime.

MAKE SURE you understand your pension plans, what your entitlements and options are in retirement, and how best to manage your plans today for maximum benefit.

GOVERNMENT PENSIONS
You may be eligible for the following pensions:

Canada Pension Plan (CPP)
The amount of your CPP benefit is based on a number of factors including the number of years you worked in Canada and the amount you contributed to the CPP over those years.

For information about current maximum CPP benefits, refer to moneycoachescanada.ca/resources.

The earliest you can apply to receive this benefit is at age 60, but your monthly benefit will be less than if you waited to start receiving it at 65. However, by starting it sooner, you might be able to leave your investments in the market for longer or spend more now while you are younger and healthier. If you apply to receive it at 70, your monthly benefit is higher than if you had started at 65. There is no financial benefit in delaying your CPP past the age of 70.

Deciding when to start taking CPP
Clients retiring early often want to know if they should start taking their CPP before they turn 65, and have a number of questions about what should factor into that decision.

The fact that CPP benefits are reduced significantly for people who opt to take it earlier creates a dilemma. Do you take the money and run? Or do you hold out until you're 65 when your CPP payments will be higher?

There's no black-and-white answer. Let's start by comparing the case of two soon-to-be retirees we'll call Joan and Chloe.

JOAN had planned to start drawing her CPP when she turned 60. She knew that for every month she took a pension ahead of her 65th birthday, her pension would be reduced by 0.6% and she'd be forfeiting 36% of what she'd otherwise receive if she waited to age 65.

Joan loves to travel and the extra money would help finance her wanderlust at a time when her health was good. So initially, the decision to take her CPP at 60 made sense to her.

While she wouldn't be making as much on her CPP as her friend Chloe - who plans to wait to age 65 - she would be collecting a pension for five years longer.

Chloe, on the other hand, has longevity in her family and determined that as long as she lived to at least age 74, she would be ahead in the overall amount of money she would have received from CPP.

After talking to her friend Chloe, Joan started worrying

that by taking a lower lifetime pension she might be missing out in the long run. She wondered if she would have enough income in her later years if she lived a long life.

What should Joan do? Take CPP at age 60 or wait until 65?

EVERY PERSON'S situation is different but here are four points to consider:

1. Your cash flow needs at age 60. If you need the money, you might want to take it now rather than waiting five years. (But don't forget to consider that you might need more money later too!)
2. Before recent changes to the CPP, it used to be you had to live to 77 to make it worthwhile waiting to collect your pension at 65. Now it's 74. Consider your needs over the years—will you have enough later to meet your cash flow needs if you take CPP early?
3. Your health. This is a huge factor but one we don't always have control over or one that we can necessarily predict. You may have health problems already at 60, or you may be like the octogenarian marathon runner. You have to make the decision that seems best for you.
4. Your personal preference. There is the 'bird in the hand' argument espoused by many that suggests taking the money now is the smarter move. Even if you don't need it, maybe you'd rather be investing the money than leaving it in the government coffers.

WHEN DECIDING on the right time to start taking CPP, there are a number of other things for you to consider:

· Your monthly CPP will increase by a larger percentage if you defer drawing it beyond age 65, although you will have to live a long time to make it worthwhile waiting to collect.
· If you decide to take your pension before 65 you can still continue working.

- Also if you're under the age of 65 and working while you get CPP, you and your employer have to continue making CPP contributions.
- If you're aged 65 to 70 and you work while drawing CPP, you can choose to continue making CPP contributions and this will increase your CPP benefits.

For more details, check out the Service Canada website at servicecanada.gc.ca.

It's important to note that many people don't qualify for the maximum CPP benefits. The average benefit paid out to retirees is 60% of the maximum.

So the first step in your CPP decision-making should be making sure you know how much you will receive. If you don't know, ask Service Canada for a Statement of Contributions. Call them at 1-800-277-9914 or sign up for your own Service Canada account through the website above. With this account you can access information on your Employment Insurance, Canada Pension Plan, and Old Age Security.

Old Age Security (OAS)

OAS is a monthly benefit available to most Canadians age 65 or older. Eligibility is based on your age and your years as a Canadian resident. The monthly OAS benefit is adjusted quarterly if the cost of living has increased as measured by the Consumer Price Index. Refer to moneycoachescanada.ca/resources for the latest OAS figures.

For low-income OAS recipients living in Canada, the Guaranteed Income Supplement (GIS) provides a monthly non-taxable benefit in addition to their OAS pension payments.

You can find out more about OAS and GIS through the same Service Canada website that links to information on the CPP.

Registered Savings

If you don't have a pension, this may be your biggest source of income.

Registered Retirement Savings Plans (RSPS)

RSPS are registered by the Canada Revenue Agency and are designed to encourage Canadians to save for retirement. Contributions to an RSP are tax-deductible at the time of investment. You defer paying tax on the money until you withdraw it. RSPS can contain investments such as stocks, bonds, mutual funds, ETFS, GICS and savings accounts.

You are allowed to contribute up to 18% of your previous year's earned income to your RSP. Any unused contribution room is carried forward indefinitely. Check your most recent notice of assessment from CRA to find out how much contribution room you have available.

Registered Retirement Income Funds (RIFS)

When you decide to start drawing a regular income from your registered savings, you are required to transfer your RSPS into RIFS (or they must be converted by December 31st of the year you turn 71). Although the packaging for your investment changes, the RIF is the same money you accumulated in your RSP and possibly the money that was previously held in a Defined Contribution Pension, if you had one. Like an RSP, you can still invest in stocks, bonds, mutual funds, GICS, savings accounts, etc. Once you convert into an RIF, you must withdraw a minimum of 5% to 20% of the balance of the RIF each year. The minimum amount is based on your (or your spouse's) age at the time of withdrawal. Withdrawals are considered taxable income.

Spousal RSPS

Spousal RSPS provide an opportunity to split future retirement income with your spouse. The contributor takes advantage of the tax savings on the contribution, but the money is invested in the name of the contributor's spouse. Eventually when money is withdrawn from the RSP or RIF, the income will be taxed in the spouse's name, at their tax rate. This usually works well when the higher-income-earning spouse makes the contribution for a lower-income spouse, thus maximizing the tax savings on the contribution and minimizing taxes payable when withdrawn later in retirement. It can also be used to even out expected retirement income between spouses to reduce the overall amount of taxes paid by a couple.

Note that the funds must be in a spousal RSP for a minimum of three years, otherwise monies withdrawn are taxed to the contributor. Recent government legislation allows for couples meeting age eligibility to split their pension income on their tax return, however, there are still some situations that make a spousal RSP an advantageous option. Talk to your tax or financial advisor.

Non-Registered Savings
At retirement, you may have some investments outside of registered accounts that you can use to provide you with an income.

Examples include: stocks, bonds, mutual funds, ETFs, GICs, savings accounts, and Tax-Free Savings Accounts.

Other Income
Use your creativity here. How else might you imagine earning income in retirement?

Examples include: Rental income, part-time employment, self-employment income etc.

ESTIMATING YOUR INCOME
Gather any pension statements that you have from the government relating to the CPP and from your employer if you have a company defined benefit pension plan. These

statements should give you an estimate of what you are entitled to at retirement. If you have been a resident of Canada for more than 10 years (after the age of 18), you will also be entitled to some of, if not the full, OAS pension.

How much income do you estimate you
will receive annually from these sources?

Defined Benefit Pension Plan $ _____

Canadian Pension Plan $ _____

Old Age Security Pension $ _____

Other Income (rental, part-
time employment etc.) $ _____

You will also receive income from your investments. This could include a defined contribution plan. Refer to balances on your most recent statements.

How much do you currently have in:

Defined Contribution Pension $ _____

Registered Savings Plans $ _____

Non-Registered Investments $ _____

How much is currently being contributed
annually to these sources?:

Defined Contribution Pension $ _____

Registered Savings Plans $ _____

Non-Registered Investments $ _____

STEP 4: How much do I have to save now?

(Otherwise known as Gap Management)

To find out how much you need to save for retirement, use the Money Coaches Canada *Financial Freedom Calculator* on our website moneycoachescanada.ca in the Resources section.

You will need the estimated annual expenses figure from your *Retirement Lifestyle Expenses* worksheet and some of the income and investment information from the previous page to plug into the calculator.

The *Financial Freedom Calculator* is required because your *Retirement Lifestyle Expenses* worksheet is in today's dollars. The calculator will factor in inflation, the estimated rate of return on your investments, when you expect to retire, and how long you expect your savings will have to last. (It is a good idea to run retirement numbers to age 95 to ensure that you don't outlive your money.)

Using the calculator you can see what happens to the numbers when you change one of the many factors (e.g., you can see the difference between how much you will need to save if you think your investments will average 4% growth or 6%, and that information might nudge you to look into different investments, or you can see how much savings you would need to retire at 55 instead of 65).

It is possible that there will be a shortfall or *gap* between how much money you estimate having in retirement (income) and how much money you think you will need to live the life you want (expenses). Don't be discouraged if there is a gap in your current plan. There usually is. The important thing is that now that you know about it, you need to plan for it and act on your plan.

Don't worry needlessly—get the facts about how much you will need to retire comfortably. Maybe you will need more money that you think. Maybe less. The only way to know for sure is to get clear about your goals and to start crunching some numbers. Get financial advice from someone you trust if you don't want to go it alone. But make a plan today—so you can enjoy tomorrow.

Other Key Retirement Planning Questions and Strategies to Consider:

Retire Your Debts Before You Do

Most people are worried about how the stock market will limit their ability to retire, but it's more likely that their debt load will be a bigger hindrance. Here's why. Debt seriously affects how much money you will need to cover your expenses in retirement. The larger your debts are, the more you will need in pensions or savings to cover those payments—on top of your living expenses.

If you are at all concerned about how your debts will affect your retirement, you are faced with two choices. You can adjust your spending today, and redirect more of your cash flow towards 'retiring your debts'—or you can plan to retire later yourself.

Target to be debt-free before retirement by setting a specific date to pay off each individual debt, one by one. If you want to retire in 10 years, adjust your payments so that your mortgage, line of credit, credit cards, and/or car loans are paid off before those 10 years are up. Don't count on making lump sum payments to pay off your debt before retirement—they simply might not happen. Adjusting your monthly payments, starting now, is much smarter and easier.

You might have to make some difficult decisions today, but by taking action steps now you will feel more in control, confident and secure when it comes time to accept your proverbial gold watch.

Do RSPs Still Make Sense?

For most people they still do. That's the short answer, but it's well worth reviewing your overall retirement strategy and the role that RSPs play in your financial decision-making.

So what are your neighbours doing about RSPs?

It's true that a lot of people are shying away from investing in RSPs, citing disappointing markets, big mortgage payments and newer TFSA options. In recent years, Statistics Canada reports that less than 25% of Canadian tax filers have been contributing to RSPs. Across Canada, the median contribution has been hovering around $3,000.

Some advisors recommend paying down your mortgage before investing in RSPs. We disagree. The problem with this strategy is that with large mortgages and longer amortization periods, by the time the debt is paid off, there is limited time to save for the income needed in retirement.

A paid-off mortgage is great, as it means lower expenses in retirement, but you still need income to cover the rest of your retirement expenses. So, unless you plan to sell your home or significantly downsize in retirement, you still need to save and invest.

In deciding whether or not it makes sense for you to invest in RSPs, here are some guidelines to consider:

· **Are you under the age of 50 and do you have 10 to 15 years left before you retire?** If the answer is yes, contributing to an RSP usually makes sense.

· **Are you in the highest income tax bracket?** For every dollar you contribute to your RSP in the highest tax bracket, you reduce your taxable income, in effect getting you a tax refund of $477 for every $1,000 you invest if you live in BC. (Tax rates vary slightly province to province.)

- **Do you have a pension plan?** If you have a pension plan through your employer, you may not be eligible to contribute much to RSPs and you may not need to if the pension meets your retirement needs.

- **Is the interest rate on your mortgage less than 4%?** If that's the case, you may be better off putting the money into an RSP than using the funds to pay down your mortgage.

- **Do you have less than $200,000 invested in RSPs?** Even if you think you'll work past 65 and your expenses are modest, you're still going to need to save and invest for retirement (unless you have a defined benefit plan).

- **Is your income less than $45,000 a year?** If your income is less than $45,000, use a TFSA instead of an RSP. You can shift the money to an RSP later if your income increases. You get a tax break for making an RSP contribution but you are taxed on every dollar when you start taking money out. So you'll want to make sure that you're getting a high enough tax break on the money you contribute.

- **Is your income likely to be considerably higher in the coming years?** Perhaps you're working part-time or you're earning what amounts to a training wage while you work towards credentials that could boost your income. It makes sense to get the largest tax break you can for your RSP contribution, so as in the case above, put your money into a TFSA and wait until you can get a refund that's ideally 30% or higher.

- **Does your employer benefit plan match RSP contributions?** Never say no to free money! If your company has any provision for matching RSP or pension contributions, take advantage of it.

- **Should you borrow to make an RSP contribution?** If you have little or no taxable income, don't borrow for an RSP. If you're in the highest tax bracket, consider borrowing but only if you don't owe money on credit cards or other high-interest debt. Borrow only if you're able to pay off your RSP loan within the year and use your tax refund to help pay off your RSP loan.

10 Ways to Get Started

We know it can be daunting to take those first steps in planning for your retirement and it often seems easier to put it off for another day. But the earlier you start, the better prepared you'll be and you'll lose the stress that comes from worrying about the unknown in your future.

Here are 10 basic—but essential—strategies and considerations to think about right now:

1. Figure out how much your lifestyle will realistically cost you in retirement.
2. Consider downsizing before you retire. (Think of it as a dress rehearsal for retirement.) Can you get by with a smaller house or just one car or less expensive vacations?
3. Pay down your debts more aggressively—starting now. Credit card loans and other such high-interest debts can add a tremendous burden on a reduced or fixed income.
4. Run some retirement income numbers including company and government pensions. Many people dismiss government pensions but they can total over $20,000 per year per person and are more secure than many people realize.
5. Become familiar with one of the newest tools to assist your retirement savings program, namely Tax-Free Savings Accounts.
6. And revisit one of the older ones—annuities. These financial products are purchased from insurance companies and are designed to provide you with peace of mind by providing you

with a safe drawdown rate through regular payments for as long as you live.

7. Consider working past age 65 or working part-time—especially if you love your job or you want to try something new.

8. Get aggressive with your savings. Even if you are in your 50s you can add substantial weight to your retirement income by saving more today. What if you took all of the income that you used to spend on your children for education, food and clothing and put that in your retirement fund?

9. Simplifying your life just might reduce your stress load and anxiety levels. Gearing down a notch or two can open you up to new possibilities of how you can live your life. Be creative in your thinking.

10. Consider doing something meaningful with your retirement years. Without the pressure of having to show up on the job every day, perhaps you could dedicate some time to making the world a better place for your grandchildren. What would that look like for you?

If you want to be confident that you are on track for a comfortable retirement, hire a financial planner or Money Coach well before your retirement date. You can crunch the numbers and create a retirement plan yourself with the help of calculators and resources available in books and on the Internet, but be sure you have the expertise, time and motivation to do it.

Our client Mary, who worried needlessly for years about whether she could ever retire, said that working with us was the best money she ever spent. Judging by the smile on her face when she got the green light for retirement, we think she meant it!

▸▸12◂◂

||||||||||||||||||||||||

BEING PREPARED
FOR EMERGENCIES

Spend 1% of your life making sure you have a solid
Plan B and 99% focused on living Plan A to the fullest.
ANONYMOUS

SO FAR, YOUR PLAN has centred on your goals; essentially that's your Plan A. But what if something should happen to you or your loved ones? It's time to spend a little bit of time on Plan B.

No one likes thinking about the potential for illness, injury, unemployment, or death but a good financial plan factors in planning for the unexpected. Neither planning nor insurance will prevent potentially difficult times, but being prepared can lessen the financial and emotional impact for you and your family.

It's easy to put off, thinking you have lots of time but your life can change in an instant and then it can be too late.

THAT HAPPENED TO our clients Liz and Bob. Their life seemed picture-perfect. A new home and a family that had prompted Liz to take a break from her work to stay home while the kids were young. Bob was the sole breadwinner for the family.

One item on their financial to-do list was getting disability insurance for Bob. Since he was self-employed and had no company plan to fall back on if illness or an accident stopped him from working, the family would have no money to live on. In their 30s, healthy and with no thought to getting sick, nonetheless they followed our advice and took out a disability insurance policy.

It was barely six months later that Bob got the dreaded diagnosis that would shatter their lives—cancer. It was a tumultuous and stressful time for the entire family, but in all their worries, there was one they could set aside—the worry over having enough money to live. Thanks to the newly acquired insurance policy, the family received regular payments that were close enough to Bob's regular income to cover their expenses.

Their story has a happy ending. Bob recovered, although it was a long and tough battle. Through it all, he had peace of mind in knowing the bills were paid and the family was averting a potential financial disaster.

PEOPLE HAVE a lot of preconceived notions about insurance, and unfortunately about insurance salespeople. Use this chapter to fill in the gaps in your knowledge and try to take a positive approach to this aspect of your financial plan.

If there's an emergency or a crisis, life is already going to be distressing and emotionally challenging. The last thing you need is to be stressed about your finances.

Emergency Fund

Start by being sure you have incorporated expenses relating to irregular, but ordinary events into your *Spending and Savings Plan*. Unexpected bills when your car breaks down, the roof leaks or the computer crashes are part of everyday life so you might as well acknowledge that and build those expenses into the plan right from the start. If you didn't make a provision for irregular events in your *Spending and Savings Plan*, go back and revisit Chapter 7.

Emergencies are the things that happen that are truly beyond regular day-to-day life. A period of unemployment, an illness, the need to help out family members—these types of events are pretty hard to anticipate and plan for but they could seriously undermine your finances and your peace of mind.

A good rule of thumb for an emergency fund is to have an amount equal to three to six months of living expenses set aside in a savings account, but it's important to delve into this further as this could potentially be a large and overwhelming number. If for example your expenses are $8,000 a month, six months' worth of expenses is almost $50,000. Easy to see why you might ignore this advice as completely unrealistic when you're barely making ends meet as it is.

A better way to approach the question of an emergency fund is to ask yourself: "If something happened to me or to my partner, would there be enough money to continue living as we are today?"

We know it may not be feasible to put aside as much as you need every month so don't think you're a total financial failure if you can't save as much as you'd like.

Some questions to consider when assessing how much your emergency fund should be:
· What are my expenses now?
· Is my job secure?
· Do I have a partner or family members who could support me if I wasn't working?
· Do I have disability insurance?
· What expenses are fixed?
· What expenses can be reduced?

Figure out what you think your cash shortfall would be if an emergency arose. Perhaps you normally set aside a lot for travel and, in an emergency like job loss or illness that could be eliminated from your expenses. But you may need to bump up your estimates due to additional medical costs or other expenses associated with emergencies. Now set a goal for how much you want to have available for your emergency fund.

MARY IS currently spending $3,000 per month. She is single, rents, doesn't own a car and has a good disability plan through her employer. She is concerned about the recent layoffs in her company, but knows that she could find a new job pretty quickly. She currently spends $500 a month on dining out and entertainment and sets aside $300 a month for travel. She could eliminate both of these expenses in an emergency, reducing her cash flow needs by $800 a month. Mary decided to set a goal of $6,600 for her emergency fund ($2,200 x 3 months).

IF YOU don't have the money to set aside right away, build an automatic monthly savings program into your *Spending and Savings Plan* and work towards your emergency fund goal. A high-interest savings account is the best place to park these funds. Even $100 a month would be a good start.

Insurance
Another way to mitigate the financial impact of a crisis is to have the right amount and the right kind of insurance.

There are various types of insurance that can help provide some financial assistance in the case of death, illness or disability. The first thing to consider is—do you actually need insurance? You have to determine, if something happens to you or to one of your loved ones, how your family finances would stand up.

Some people may have sufficient assets, resources and income from other sources without having to rely on insurance but for most people and families, some form of insurance is usually required.

When should you be looking at your insurance needs?

You can buy insurance at any time of life, provided you have the financial means and you meet the eligibility requirements. Listed below are times when it would be especially wise to review your needs. You may or may not need to make a change at any of these junctures, but thinking about your insurance, and other aspects of your financial plan at these key times is a good habit to get into.

Buying a new home: Often a couple buying a new house will consider buying life insurance policies. If either were to die, or become unable to earn an income due to illness or injury, the other person could need financial assistance to make the mortgage payments and remain in the home.

Paying off your mortgage: Once you're clear of major debts and your shelter is secure, you may consider reducing your insurance coverage. Your living expenses drop significantly when you no longer have to make mortgage payments, so depending on the other circumstances in your life, you and your dependents, if any, may require less financial resources.

Making a life commitment: If either you or your partner would be financially disadvantaged by the lack of the other's income, you might consider insurance at this time. However, if you both have a strong potential to earn, no dependents and no major debts to burden the other partner, you would need to weigh the cost of insurance against the benefits.

Getting divorced or being widowed: You will need to adjust your policies if your spouse was the beneficiary. You may also want to look into forms of insurance that provide you with financial support if you become unable to take care of yourself or your dependents due to illness or injury. And if you received insurance coverage through your spouse's benefit plan, you will need to look at replacing that coverage.

Having children or other dependents: Parents are wise to ensure that they have a financial backup plan to replace the contribution that they make to support their children and other family members. If you have an aging parent, sibling or someone who is financially dependent on you, you also need to consider them when you review your insurance needs.

Having self-sufficient children or becoming dependent-free: When dependents no longer need you for their financial survival, your life expenses shift, so you might consider reducing your insurance. However, as they age, some people look at life insurance as a way of securing a legacy, or reducing the tax burden when their children inherit their assets.

Starting or closing a business: In either case, you will likely have specific insurance needs. And you may also require personal insurance to be eligible for a business loan.

Life Insurance

The main reason that people buy life insurance is because their current income is supporting the lifestyle of people they care about and without that income, their family or partners would suffer financially.

You don't buy life insurance for yourself. You buy it for your beneficiary.

When the policy holder dies, the insurance company pays a lump sum to the beneficiary named in the policy. It is very important to keep this information up to date. If you have remarried, but your ex-partner is still named as your beneficiary, the insurance company has no choice but to pay your ex. If you name a child, and then have a second child, you may want to add both names to the policy. Or, if your beneficiary dies before you do, you will need to name someone else.

When choosing a beneficiary for your policy, try to imagine who will be financially responsible for your funeral arrangements, your debts, or your dependents.

In Canada, the money someone receives as a beneficiary of a life insurance policy is not taxable. So if you purchase a policy worth $500,000, your beneficiary should receive the full $500,000 when you die.

THERE ARE TWO BASIC FORMS OF LIFE INSURANCE:

Term Insurance

The sole purpose of buying term life insurance is to leave someone a guaranteed amount of money when you die. It is not a savings vehicle and it has no cashable value if it is cancelled, or if it lapses.

You purchase this form of life insurance in limited terms e.g. five, 10 or 20 years.

It is relatively inexpensive when you are young and healthy, but when you renew the policy, you will likely pay an increased rate for each new term.

GROUP INSURANCE, provided as a benefit through your employer, is a type of term insurance that usually ends when you stop working for your employer. You may be able to convert your policy into private term insurance outside a group plan. Be sure to check rates and limits to new coverage.

MORTGAGE INSURANCE is also a form of term insurance. It is offered by most lending institutions and it pays the balance of your mortgage to the lending institution if a person listed on the mortgage dies. The premiums are set based on the amount of money you owe at the time of issuing the policy. But the value of your debt decreases over time. Therefore, the amount of insurance coverage that you are paying for decreases. However, your premium stays the same. Shop around and compare the cost of mortgage insurance to the cost of other life insurance options.

Whole Life / Universal Life Insurance
These policies have a life insurance component and an investment component. With each contribution, a portion pays for your insurance premium and the other portion is invested.

With a whole life policy, you pay level premiums for a specified number of years. In the early years of the policy, the chances that you will die are significantly lower. So, the premiums you pay exceed the actual cost of covering you. The insurance company invests these excess payments (on your behalf) to cover the increasing cost of insuring you as you get older.

WITH UNIVERSAL LIFE, you choose the size of premiums and the payment period based on an assumed rate of return on the investments within the policy. Whole life and universal life policies are said to have a cash value, because if you cancel the policy, any money that has accrued in your investments is yours to remove. (There may be a cancellation fee, or redemption charge.)

These policies are often more expensive to start, but if you hold the policy long enough, you should reach a point where the policy has enough cash reserves to pay your future premiums.

This form of life insurance is often chosen by people who know they will need life insurance well into old age and beyond, for instance someone with a lifelong dependent or with specialized estate tax issues. It may also be of interest to people who are looking for additional tax advantaged savings if they have paid off their mortgage and maximized their RSP contributions.

How do I buy life insurance?

Life insurance is available through insurance brokers or agents, banks and credit unions. You may also have, or be able to buy, life insurance through your company, alumni association or professional association.

How much does it cost?

Premiums for life insurance are dependent on your age, gender, health, smoking status, the term you choose and the amount of coverage you want to purchase.

Currently, for a non-smoking, healthy 40 year old woman, premiums for a 10-year term policy of $500,000 would be in the range of $30 to $35 per month. For a non-smoking, healthy 40 year old male, premiums for the same type of policy would be in the $40 to $45 per month range. If all else is equal, life insurance premiums tend to be lower for women because they are expected to live longer.

Who buys it?

Couples, parents, new home owners, and new business owners tend to buy life insurance, but it is important to remember that the amount they buy will likely change over the course of a lifetime. You may need more when you have a young family, no savings and/or a large debt. Typically, life insurance needs decline as you accumulate assets and/or your dependents become independent.

If you are single, unless you have dependents, significant debts, or a burning desire to leave a financial legacy, you may not need life insurance. However, some singles do choose to secure life insurance coverage while they are young and healthy in anticipation of their future needs.

Disability Insurance

Most people hear a lot more about life insurance than disability insurance, but disability insurance is a very important type of insurance to consider.

One of the most valuable assets you have today is your ability to earn income. A disability could impede your ability to work, so the risk of illness and injury is a significant risk to your financial security. Disability insurance can provide you with a monthly income if you cannot work.

As long as you are alive, you are going to need money, and if you aren't physically or mentally able to earn it, you need to know where it will come from. Personal savings is one option. Government assistance is minimal. Depending on family and loved ones might be an option. Disability insurance can pay as much as 85% of your current income, on a monthly basis.

But not all policies are equal so it is important to read the policy options carefully. Make sure you're clear on what constitutes a disability; how long you have to be disabled before the benefits begin and how long the benefits will continue to be paid out.

Where do I get disability insurance?

Many employers provide some type of disability insurance, but don't assume it's included in your benefits package or that what is provided will be sufficient for your needs.

If you don't have sufficient coverage through your employer or if you are self-employed, be sure to talk to a licensed insurance agent or broker.

How much does it cost?

Disability insurance premiums are calculated based on a variety of considerations including: amount and term of coverage, age, gender, income, health, and occupation. Premiums can vary significantly from policy to policy.

To give you an idea, when Karin was 41, she bought a disability policy worth $3,000/month (plus inflation) to age 65. She pays monthly premiums of $156. That may seem high, but if she were disabled at age 45, the policy would pay Karin $36,000 a year for 20 years, and cost the insurance company over a million dollars.

If you don't have a financial backup plan, you really need to consider the value of disability insurance.

Who buys it?

A lot of people buy it for a lot of different reasons. Single people buy it in the hopes of remaining self-sufficient if they become disabled. Couples buy it so that neither person will have to bear the full financial responsibility for their household. Parents buy it to make sure they can continue to support their children and themselves. Self-employed people buy it because they don't have company benefits such as sick leave and extended medical leave. Employed people buy it because their benefits may not include an extended sick leave, or their disability benefits might be limited.

The only people who are unlikely to consider disability insurance would be people who don't earn an income, or people who are financially independent.

Tax considerations

The way your disability insurance premiums are paid determines how the government will tax you, should you ever be paid an income from the policy.

If you pay your own disability premiums, either directly to your insurer or to your employer, any monthly benefits you receive will be tax-free.

If your employer pays your premiums, any monthly benefits you receive are considered taxable income, so if you have a policy that pays you $36,000 a year, you will have to pay taxes out of that income.

If you are self-employed, we recommend that you don't deduct your disability premiums as a business expense. If you do use the premiums as a deduction, you'll have to pay tax on the monthly benefit if you ever need to make a claim.

Critical Illness Insurance

Critical illness insurance is still relatively new in Canada. It is designed to pay you a guaranteed lump sum amount of money if you become critically ill. Unlike disability insurance, your ability to earn an income is not an issue; your specific diagnosis is the issue.

What is a critical illness?

Different insurers, and different policies, may define critical illness differently, so review your options carefully. Generally speaking, a critical illness is a life-threatening medical condition, such as life-threatening forms of cancer, stroke or heart attack.

How does critical illness Insurance work?

Critical illness insurance pays out the full value of your policy in a lump sum 30 days after you're diagnosed, if you survive. This payment would not be taxable. You can use the money any way you choose. For example, you might choose to invest the lump sum and live off of the income, rest comfortably on a beach in Mexico, pay off debts, or pay for treatments or procedures not covered by your basic medical coverage.

Who buys it?

Critical illness coverage is becoming popular with single people because they're less likely to have someone in their life who could support them financially if they became critically ill.

Also people who aren't eligible for disability insurance, either because they're already disabled or because they work in a high-risk occupation may still be eligible for critical illness insurance. Critical illness insurance could be an option for anyone who foresees the need for cash in the event of a critical illness.

You must be between the ages of 18 and 65 with an acceptable medical history to qualify. The more likely you are to experience a critical illness, the higher your premiums; and it's possible that you wouldn't be approved for coverage at all.

How much does it cost?
You can purchase any amount, from $25,000 to $2 million. Costs depend on your age, family history, smoking status, and medical history. The cost is also based on the number of critical illnesses you want covered.

Some policies give you the option to get your premiums back if you cancel the policy before using it. And some will pay out to your estate if you die before claiming. These options may have higher premiums.

Long-Term Care Insurance
This is also relatively new in Canada. Long-Term Care Insurance is designed to provide benefits to people who require private facility care, or home care, on a long-term basis.

Currently, the cost of private, long-term care facilities ranges between $2,000 and $8,000 a month. That's significantly more than many people would otherwise budget for their shelter. Some home care is provided by the government, but many people who wish to remain in their home have to pay for additional care. The trend towards hiring professional caregivers means that people need to plan for significant health-related expenses. Long-term care insurance could be part of that plan.

How does long-term care insurance work?

In order to claim on the policy, you have to be unable to perform two activities of daily living, such as: feeding, dressing, bathing, toileting, or cognitive activities.

Who buys it?

People who do not qualify for critical illness or disability insurance might consider long-term care insurance. People who have assets that are important to their family, like a family home, may be concerned about having to sell the asset should they need long-term care. For those people, this insurance could provide assurance that they won't have to sell their assets. You must be over the age of 18 to purchase it.

How much does it cost?

Costs are based on the amount of monthly benefit you want, how long you want the benefit to last (for a set term or for your lifetime), and whether or not you choose to have a monthly payment policy, or a reimbursement policy, meaning that you submit receipts for reimbursement. At this time, many companies are not guaranteeing premiums for more than five years.

What Are Your Basic Insurance Needs?

Everyone is different. These questions will help you start to consider your financial needs at death, or in the event of injury or illness. Refer back to your *Spending and Savings Plan* to see where specific costs might go up or down. In the event of a death of a spouse, the rule of thumb is that you will need 75% of the family's current income. In the event of illness or disability, your monthly expenses are most likely to go up.

How much income would you, or your family, need to replace?

If you die: $ _____ per year

If you are disabled: $ _____ per year

If your spouse dies: $ _____ per year

If your spouse is disabled: $ _____ per year

How much debt would you,
or your family, need to pay off? $ _____

What additional expenses might you, or your family,
need to pay?

If you or your spouse dies: _____
e.g. funeral, child care, medical assistance

If you or your spouse is disabled: _____
e.g. medical assistance, home renovations

Thinking about Life Insurance needs...
ANN is a stay at home mom with two infants. Her husband is the only income earner. If he died, she would need: $200,000 to pay off the mortgage, $40,000 annually for 10 years to cover her expenses, and save for her retirement and the kids' education, $25,000 for the funeral, legal and other costs. Their insurance agent calculated that her husband would need a $577,400 term life insurance policy to cover her needs.

Thinking about Disability Insurance needs...
TERI AND SUE both earn about $70,000. They have a son in school and a mortgage. If either were disabled, they would still need to pay the mortgage, pay for child care, cover their monthly expenses, save for the future and pay additional health costs. Both women have disability insurance for

60% of their current income. They are comfortable that it's enough to maintain a good quality of life.

Review, Revise and Take Action

The thing about insurance is that you really never know when you're going to need it. You don't want to be in a position where something has happened and you wish that you had gotten around to making a change or buying a policy.

SADLY THAT happened to Jim and Ginny, clients who had recently bought a house and were just starting their life together. Jim had a life insurance policy through his employer, but like many people, he originally signed up for it at a time when he was still single. Asked to name a beneficiary, he, like many young people named his parents.

They left one of our sessions with a task list—one of the items was to change the beneficiary on Jim's life insurance. He never did get the time. Tragically, he was killed in an accident and the insurance payout went to the named beneficiary (his parents), not Ginny. Suddenly alone and with no insurance to cover the mortgage, she was forced to sell their home.

SO SIMPLY having an insurance policy in place isn't enough. You'll want to make sure it's updated and appropriate to the changing circumstances in your life.

Before you buy insurance, review the coverage that you, and/or your spouse, already have and note any gaps or questions. If you're part of a group plan at work, don't assume it gives you all the coverage you require. Talk to the provider, or read your benefit booklet to make sure you understand your coverage and your benefits. If you or your spouse has personal insurance, ask yourself, and possibly your provider, if it is still the right policy for your current circumstances.

Review your named beneficiaries. Make sure all your policies have up-to-date beneficiaries named. If they need to be changed, mark that as an immediate 'to-do' on your calendar.

If you decide that you need to buy insurance:
Find an agent you trust. Referrals are particularly important when it comes to buying insurance for a very simple reason. People dislike talking about death, illness and injury. That's not surprising. So look for an agent who puts you at ease. If you're comfortable with your agent, you will be that much more likely to call him or her when you need to adjust your policy.

Ask your financial advisor if he or she is licensed to sell insurance. If so, it might be to your advantage to buy insurance from someone who knows your full financial story.

Ask how your insurance agent gets paid. Generally you don't pay an agent, the insurance provider does. Some insurance agents receive a commission when they sell a product, and they may or may not receive a fee from the insurance provider after that. Be wary of an agent who regularly suggests new and better policies unless you can see clear benefits for the change.

Manage your risks. This means making sure that you have plans to cover the greatest risks to you and to your family. Identify which types of insurance should be a top priority for you and which you might add later. Keep in mind your health could become an eligibility factor.

Update your Spending and Savings Plan. Insurance can be expensive, but it's often necessary to help you to live the life you want. So don't forget to factor it into your *Spending and Savings Plan*.

While it's unsettling to think about the curveballs that life throws at us, having an emergency fund and the right insurance coverage will help you sleep at night knowing that you and your family will be well taken care of financially.

▸▸13◂◂

||||||||||||||||||||||||

LEGAL
MATTERS

In this world nothing can be said
to be certain, except death and taxes.
BENJAMIN FRANKLIN

YOU MIGHT NOT want to think about Wills and estate planning but you are too far down the path to financial control to give up now. This chapter will help you plan and protect those you love.

Estate Planning

We have suggested you seek professional advice in other chapters, but we can't stress enough how important it is to get legal and financial help from estate planning professionals. As Money Coaches, we have seen the family nightmares that can happen when estate planning is not properly considered. Save your family strife; plan and protect.

And note there are unique tax considerations specific to estate planning. Talk to your investment and tax advisors to ensure that your plans factor in any taxes that might be passed on with your estate assets.

What is Estate Planning?

Estate planning may sound grand, but it just means that you have made plans for what you want to happen when you die, if you are incapacitated, or near death. Essentially, it's a gift you can prepare while you're alive for the people or organizations you leave behind.

Your estate is everything you own: personal effects, real estate, investments, insurance policies, intellectual property rights, licences and other business property, etc. Your estate also includes your debt.

It is critical that you make the necessary decisions and prepare the necessary documents now. If you don't, there may be no way for your wishes to be carried out. Worse yet, the legacy you leave could be a financial and legal battle.

Key estate planning questions
- Who will be primarily responsible for carrying out your wishes upon death, or if you become unable to manage your affairs?
- Have you provided direction for your medical treatment, organ donation and funeral arrangements?
- Have you left enough money to cover your funeral expenses, or have you prepaid them?
- Does anyone know what type of burial and funeral arrangements you would like?
- Do you plan to die broke? Or do you want to plan to leave an income or inheritance to loved ones?
- Do you have plans to cover debts you might have?
- Who will inherit your estate? How will it be divided? Would you like to include a charity?
- Have you made arrangements for any beneficiaries with special needs?
- Have you made arrangements for children of a previous marriage?
- Do you need to make arrangements for someone to assume guardianship of your children?
- Do you have plans to transfer your business so that it survives after you die?

Make Your Wishes Clear

You need a Will. A Will is a legal document that leaves instructions about what you want done with your estate.

It can save your family a tremendous amount of grief and headache. You may not think it could happen in your family, but the combination of intense emotion and money can turn even the most functional families into feuding and angry antagonists. The best way to minimize this risk is by being very clear and specific in your intentions upon death, and by having those wishes drafted into a legal Will.

What happens if I die without a Will?

If you die without a Will, someone, usually a spouse or adult child, needs to file legal documents asking the court to appoint him or her to settle your estate. If there is no one who can settle the estate, the Public Trustee takes responsibility and laws determine who will inherit. As a result, an estranged spouse, or a family member you didn't know existed could inherit everything.

The bottom line is, without a Will you have no control over who gets what.

Where do I go to get a Will?

A Will can be drawn up by a lawyer, or other legal professionals like a notary or notary public or you can do it yourself. However, we strongly encourage you to work with a legal professional because it's imperative that a Will is drafted, signed and initialed correctly, otherwise it could be considered invalid.

For most people, the cost of having a Will drawn up is money well spent. But you can keep costs down by deciding on the key points before seeing a legal professional.

Your Will should clearly state: Who you appoint as executor, who you will leave your money and possessions to, and if you have dependent children, who will be their guardian. Burial instructions can also be included.

What assets are not included in my Will?

- Any asset that has a named beneficiary falls outside the juris-diction of your Will because you have already established who will inherit the asset.
- RSPs, insurance policies, and pensions give you the option of naming a beneficiary. If a beneficiary is named, the asset bypasses the Will.
- If you have bank accounts, non-registered investments and real estate assets in joint names (with 'right of survivorship'), at death, those assets should roll over to the other person named, so these assets don't need to be included in your Will.

AND REMEMBER, it is up to you to keep the beneficiaries named on these assets up to date. If your Will simply says that you want your son to inherit your estate, but your sister is still the named beneficiary on your RSP from the days before you had a child, you could accidentally give a large chunk of your assets to the wrong person.

Probate

Probate is the legal process that confirms the validity of a Will. It takes time and it costs money but in most cases it has to be done.

It is the responsibility of the executor to initiate the probate process. Though it can be done by the executor alone, it is a complicated process and it's usually done by a legal professional.

Once a Will has been through probate, financial institutions and the executor can begin the process of distributing the assets of the estate.

Unless the estate has minimal assets, it's not generally possible to avoid probating the Will. While it may be desirable to avoid or minimize probate fees, it shouldn't be your only estate planning concern. However, people often plan to have some assets outside the Will, such as life insurance policies, so they can go directly to the named beneficiary without delay or probate fees.

Who Will Speak For You When You Can No Longer Speak For Yourself?

THE EXECUTOR

An executor is the person you appoint to carry out the instructions of your Will. You could choose a family member, a trusted friend, a business partner, or a professional (e.g., your lawyer). You could also choose an institution, such as a trust company.

Ideally, you want to choose someone who is likely to outlive you, and who lives in your city or town, so that administrative duties don't require that person to make multiple or long journeys. Also, this is a diplomatic and detail-oriented job. Depending on your family dynamics, you may be able to count on a specific family member, or you may see advantages to asking someone outside the immediate family to take the role. An executor can be paid a fee. You can stipulate this specifically in your Will, or the executor can claim up to 5% of the estate value with the permission of the beneficiaries.

The duties of the executor include:
· Completing funeral arrangements
· Having your Will probated and distributing assets to your beneficiaries
· Paying your debts
· Completing your income tax return
· Applying for the Canada Pension Plan death benefit

POWER OF ATTORNEY

A Will only becomes valid upon death. But what happens if you are incapacitated and can't handle your financial affairs? Even if you are married, your spouse can't just step in unless your bank accounts, investments or real estate assets are in joint names.

Power of Attorney allows someone to make financial and legal decisions for you, and sign financial documents on your behalf if you're unable to do so due to accident, illness, or absence. Without a legal declaration, no one, not even your spouse or your parents, can sign for you.

Each province has its own laws around Powers of Attorney so it's important to determine the requirements in your province. Generally, Power of Attorney doesn't cover personal care or medical decisions, although depending where you live, that may not be the case. For example, under New Brunswick law, Power of Attorney can cover personal care as well as property and financial decisions.

Power of Attorney is a powerful document that gives the person you appoint significant rights and responsibilities. Unless your attorney is your spouse, it's best to keep your Power of Attorney document with your lawyer, with instructions to release the document to your appointed attorney only if medical or other pre-stated conditions are met. You may want to appoint two people to act as 'co-attorneys' to avoid potential abuses, but make sure you pick two people who can work together.

REPRESENTATION AGREEMENTS AND LIVING WILLS

Depending on where you live in Canada, your wishes for your medical care should you become too ill or incapacitated to make decisions for yourself can be outlined in a Living Will, a Representation Agreement, an Advance Health Care Directive or similar document. Without such advance planning and appropriate documentation, decisions concerning your body and life could be made by people who don't know, or respect, your wishes. If you're in a medical situation where you are considered by medical staff to be unable to make decisions about your care, by law, they have to ask your family for instruction.

IF YOU HAVE no family, decisions about your care will go before the Public Guardian and Trustee unless you have legally named a representative. Make sure you know the laws for your province and ensure that you have the legal documentation you need to ensure decisions about your health and personal care are made by the person you choose.

For example, if you want to ensure that no extraordinary measures are used to keep you alive (if in a coma or dying from a terminal illness), you need to make sure that the representative you name will have the legal authority to see your wishes are followed.

Being clear about your wishes, and who you trust to speak for you, can prevent serious family disputes over medical treatment decisions.

Talk While You Still Can

It may be difficult to talk to people about your plans, but it's much better for everyone if you do.

Ultimately, you want decisions about your assets, your medical treatments and potentially your death, to be your own. And it's important to recognize that it could be difficult for family members to fully appreciate your wishes if they're in crisis. So talking with them and writing a clear plan now gives you an opportunity to address their concerns and express your point of view.

Tell the appropriate people where your financial and legal documents are kept. Make sure they know who your lawyer and financial advisors are. If people don't know you have made plans, the plans won't do you much good unless your lawyer just happens to attend your bedside.

If you are named in someone else's estate plan (your partner, children, or parents) make sure you understand your responsibilities and talk to them about their wishes, so you can respect them.

'Til Divorce Do Us Part

Death and serious illness are not the only life events that can derail your well-organized financial plans.

While there's no getting around the hurt and pain of separation or divorce, understanding the financial implications of a break-up can save you time, money, and grief. And the sooner you consider how your finances will be affected, the better. If your spouse handled the money in the family, it's crucial you begin your financial education well before you start your legal negotiations so you can level the playing field.

Here are six financial action steps to consider as soon as you know separation or divorce is likely:

1. Ask for help. Although you might have to bring in lawyers, accountants or actuaries at some later point, your immediate financial priority is to find a trusted friend, relative, or professional financial advisor to serve as a financial support person—someone who can help keep you balanced and focused.

2. Prioritize. With the help of your support person, prioritize your financial concerns and issues. Making a simple priority list is not only practical it also helps minimize the strong emotions that might otherwise cloud your judgment. Ask yourself: "Do I have enough cash available to cover basic expenses—and for how long? What bills are urgent—rent or mortgage payments, child care expenses, insurance payments—and what can wait? What expenses need to be

covered in the near future (postdated cheques, scheduled bank withdrawals, tax payments)?"

3. Determine what professional financial or legal assistance you might need, once you have dealt with your immediate financial needs. Do you already have an independent financial advisor to help you? If not, ask for referrals—ideally from someone who has recently been separated and is in a similar financial situation to you. The same goes for a lawyer.

4. Collect all your financial information before meeting with potential advisors. That includes assets (cash, bank accounts, real estate, household effects, vehicles, investment accounts and stock certificates, RSPs, pension plans and other investments, receivables, business interests, and inheritances) and liabilities (bills, mortgage, lines of credit, credit cards, personal loans, car loans and leases) held separately or jointly with your spouse or partner. Make sure the information is as up-to-date as possible. Summarize your assets and liability information by creating a *Net Worth Statement* so you have a full picture of your finances.

5. Consider what your expenses will be when you are living on your own. Start by looking at how much you have spent in the past then make adjustments for your change in circumstances. Collect this information on a *Spending and Savings Plan* worksheet.

6. Locate recent tax returns, life insurance policies, Wills and Powers of Attorney, safety deposit boxes and other legal documents. You will need this information for your advisors and to update your post-divorce financial plan.

Have your financial advisor help you figure out what type of financial settlement you will need to protect your financial security. Then work with your lawyer to figure out what's possible legally and how best to divide assets.

Divorce is traumatic no matter how much goodwill is still remaining or how much money is at stake. The decisions you make during this time can have a significant impact on your future financial security so take the time to educate yourself and refuse to be pressured or rushed into important financial decisions.

Prenuptial Agreements

While a prenuptial agreement may not ease the trauma of a break-up, it can help forestall a drawn-out dispute that could potentially drain family finances.

Prenuptial agreements used to be just for the rich and famous but an increasing number of brides and grooms are signing prenups. There are many and varied reasons, including children from a previous marriage, business ownership, estate planning, one partner bringing in considerable debt or conversely, bringing in considerable assets. Prenups or cohabitation agreements as they are sometimes called may also be a good idea if you plan to live together even if you don't plan to marry. A family lawyer can advise you on what's best for your particular circumstances.

It's a good idea to get a prenup, particularly if there is an imbalance in terms of assets coming to the table. For instance if one of the partners has significant net worth and the other one doesn't, it's particularly important to have a prenup that states your desires about the arrangements that are comfortable to both of you.

If you want to do anything in the event of divorce that is potentially unique to your own circumstances and doesn't fall under the default provisions of the law, then it's best to be proactive by drafting a prenup.

You may be reluctant to have this discussion with your partner-to-be but if you feel you can't bring up the question of money, you'd better be careful. If you can't talk about money before you are married or move in together, that could be a real danger sign.

LIKE ALL the potential emergencies and crises covered in the last two chapters, it may seem easiest to just ignore potential pitfalls and hope they never happen. But being prepared will give you the most peace of mind.

TAKE
CONSCIOUS
ACTION

▸▸14◂◂

‖‖‖‖‖‖‖‖‖‖‖‖‖‖‖‖‖‖‖‖‖

JUST
DO IT

*A little knowledge that acts is worth
infinitely more than much knowledge that is idle.*

KAHLIL GIBRAN

YOU SHOULD NOW have a better understanding of the basics of personal finances—what areas of your money you have under control and what areas still need some work.

You might be confident that you have a healthy relationship with money, but you need to work on setting up a better system for saving. Or you may have your cash flow under control, but you want to learn more about your investments. Maybe you still have some money habits that you need help correcting.

If you've been living with financial challenges for years, there are no quick fixes. And you don't have to have everything under control immediately. You just need to make a commitment to yourself that you will keep working on your plan, you will keep asking questions and you will do what you can to take control of your money.

Take Conscious Action Now

It's time to put the knowledge you have about yourself and your money into action. It's now up to you to take the appropriate, conscious action to take charge of your money and start living the life you want.

We have given you tips and tools to help you get organized and focused, but only you can take the *conscious action* required to take the next step with your money.

You are taking conscious action when you:
· Clarify your goals and act on your intentions
· Ask questions and further your financial education
· Check in with yourself and exercise your awareness
· Spend and save your money with intention, education and awareness
· Seek professional assistance to help you move closer to your ideal life

What next steps do you need to take to feel more fully empowered and on track with your money? Do you have a list of action items to complete? Are there phone calls, or appointments, you need to make to follow through on your plans?

Complete the *Financial Plan Checklist* on the next page so that you have a quick reference list of what you have done, and what you have left to do.

And use the *Action Plan* page to consolidate your to-do lists. List anything you need to do to complete your plan, or to move your plan into action. The key to the *Action Plan* is to be specific and set deadlines for yourself. You may even want to put your *Action Plan* up on your fridge, or keep a copy of it in your daytimer to remind you of to-do items.

FINANCIAL PLAN CHECKLIST

	Yes	No	Don't Know
1. Have you written down your Life and Financial Goals?	☐	☐	☐
2. Do you know what your Net Worth is?	☐	☐	☐
3. Have you prepared your Spending and Savings Plan?	☐	☐	☐
4. Are you regularly saving towards your goals?	☐	☐	☐
5. Do you have an emergency fund or personal line of credit?	☐	☐	☐
6. Do you pay your credit cards in full every month?	☐	☐	☐
7. Do you have an investment strategy that is appropriate for your goals and your risk tolerance?	☐	☐	☐
8. Do you understand how to read your investment statements? (If not, now is the time to book an appointment with your advisor!)	☐	☐	☐
9. Are you saving for your retirement every year?	☐	☐	☐
10. Are you on track for your retirement goals?	☐	☐	☐
11. Are you confident that you are taking advantage of all the tax deductions that you are entitled to?	☐	☐	☐
12. Do you have adequate life insurance?	☐	☐	☐
13. Do you have adequate disability, critical illness and/or long-term care insurance?	☐	☐	☐
14. Are your beneficiaries up to date on your RSPs, pensions and insurance policies?	☐	☐	☐
15. Do you have a good understanding of your pension and insurance programs with your employer?	☐	☐	☐
16. Do you have an up-to-date Will, Power of Attorney and Health Care Directive?	☐	☐	☐
17. Do you know what you need to do to achieve your financial goals?	☐	☐	☐

ACTION PLAN

If you answered No or Don't Know to any of the questions on the *Financial Plan Checklist* you will need an *Action Plan* to achieve your goals. Your *Action Plan* should be very specific with a time frame assigned to each item on your list.

REMEMBER: *Goals are dreams with a deadline.*
Dreams without a deadline are just wishes.

	ACTION STEP	TIME FRAME
☐		
☐		
☐		
☐		
☐		
☐		

FOR EXAMPLE:

	ACTION STEP	TIME FRAME
√	Review my action steps	Today
√	Schedule an hour a month to work on finances	Today
√	Set up a savings account for my priority goals	Monday on my lunch break
√	Book an appointment with my investment advisor to review investments and to increase my RSP contribution	by Friday
	Update my Will	by December 31
	Find a friend to keep me motivated, and on track with my finances	Before New Year
	Continue to learn about finances	Register for Money Mondays

Review and Revise

As a general rule, keep in mind that you need to review and revise your plan and strategies to address your changing needs, goals, and overall financial position. This is especially important if you have significant changes in your life, such as marriage, divorce, having children, or retirement.

The good news is that as life shifts and changes, you can use what you have learned here to systematically ensure that your money will continue to support you in the next stage of your life.

To be sure you are staying on track with your money, use the *My Annual Review Checklist* every year *(see following page)*. Complete it either at the end of the year, at tax time, or whenever you do your goal-setting for the year.

Getting Back on Track

There are a few typical stumbling blocks that could derail your best intentions. You may take on too much at once or you might hit a roadblock, such as an unsatisfactory meeting with an advisor, trying to meet unrealistic expectations or a disagreement with your partner that leaves you discouraged. You might forget to schedule time in the calendar to deal with your finances or fall back into some of your old financial habits.

Don't be too discouraged if this happens to you. The solution is to be patient but firm with yourself. Go back to your goals and think about your reasons for taking charge of your finances in the first place. See how far you've come. If a crisis is throwing you off, remind yourself that you aren't always in control of how life unfolds and go back to your plan.

Sticking with your game plan will contribute to your financial joy and ease and you'll know that you're doing the best you can with your finances to move towards the kind of life you want to live now and in the future.

MY ANNUAL REVIEW CHECKLIST

☐ **Review and revise your life & financial goals**
Have major life events changed your goals?
How far have you come?

_____

☐ **Update your Net Worth Statement**
Has your Net Worth improved since last year?
Why or why not?

_____

☐ **Update your Spending and Savings Plan**
Are you following your *Spending and Savings Plan*?
What have been the challenges? Successes?

_____

☐ **Review your savings for your priority goals**
Are you regularly contributing to your savings as planned?
Are you satisfied with how much you have saved for your
goals?
Could you contribute more now?
Do you have an emergency fund?

_____

☐ **Review your debt**
Are you debt-free?
Do you have a date that you want to be debt-free by?
Are you paying your credit cards in full every month?
Are you paying down your debt as you had planned?

_____

☐ **Review your investment Statements**
Review your asset allocation.
Are you investing as planned?
Is your asset mix still appropriate for your goals?

☐ **Review your Retirement Plan**
Are you clear about what you need to save for retirement?
Are you saving enough to meet your retirement goals?
How much do you have in your RSP now?
Are you maximizing your pension benefits?
Are your named beneficiaries up to date on your pension(s)
and RSP?

☐ **Meet your financial advisor to review your investments**
Have you found an advisor you like working with?
Are you on track with your investment goals?
Are you on track with your retirement goals?
Do you need to rebalance or adjust your asset allocation?

☐ **Review your insurance policies**
Do you have adequate life insurance?
Are your beneficiaries up to date on your life insurance?
Do you have adequate insurance to cover your lifestyle and
savings needs should you become disabled or unable to work
due to illness?

☐ **Review your Estate Plan**
Do you have an up-to-date Will, Power of Attorney, Health
Care Directive?

Unstuck and Living the Life you Want

In the end, though, it's all very simple. Do these things and you can get ahead financially and start living the life you want.

1. Be honest with yourself about the role that money plays in your life (past and now)

· Know you're not alone—it's hard for all of us to withstand the impact of cultural and family influences.
· A better understanding of beliefs and attitudes brings more understanding, acceptance and compassion.
· Having more awareness reduces the fear of engaging with money.
· You'll be happier because you'll be aware of the influences that have contributed to negative habits and beliefs and you can take action to make changes.

2. Take a proactive role with your money and try to become more comfortable talking about money

· Don't stop learning; keep up your financial education. Consider taking courses, working with a financial advisor or Money Coach, taking part in an investment group, keeping updated on personal finance issues through blogs and news stories. It will help build your confidence and increase your sense of control over your finances.
· Talk about money with your spouse, friends and family.
· Be open to changing your money habits and set intentions for having a different relationship with money.
· You'll be happier because you'll feel more confident and in control.

3. Be clear about what you want going forward in terms of your values and goals

· Create a vision and set authentic goals; you'll likely find you have more power and potential than you thought.
· Well-defined, clearly articulated goals are easier to achieve.

- Focusing on your top three priority goals will simplify your life.
- You'll be happier because you'll know where you're going and you'll be more energized and motivated to do what it takes to get what you want.

4. Have a plan for today
- You will be more resourceful and creative at finding solutions when you know where you stand.
- Creating a basic plan with goals, your *Net Worth Statement* and a *Spending and Savings Plan* will help you define and clarify your goals; figure out where you are now; and take steps to get what you want.
- Knowledge is power.
- You'll be happier because you'll feel like you're in control; you won't feel like money is running your life; you'll have money in your accounts before you need it and you won't be adding to your debt load so you'll feel you have more freedom.

5. Have a plan for tomorrow
- Understand the basics of investing and build a goal-centred investment plan.
- Understand what you're investing in and develop a pro-active relationship with your investment advisor.
- Know how much you need to save, invest, and do now to meet the retirement plan that you've mapped out for your future.
- Figure out how much is enough for you. Be realistic about what's possible and absolutely necessary and what are extras.
- You'll be happier because you'll know that you're okay or at least you'll know what you need to do to have a secure future.

6. Be prepared for the unexpected
- Have a plan.
- Have an emergency fund.
- Have adequate insurance.

- Have a Will, Power of Attorney and Health Care Directive in place.
- You'll be happier because you'll know that you and your family are taken care of when unexpected events happen.

7. Take charge and make it happen
- Be honest with yourself. There are no quick solutions and it might not be your favourite way to spend your time, but taking control of your finances will allow you to live better.
- Once you get into it, the rewards—both financial and emotional can be so immediate and tangible that you'll find it's worth the effort.
- Create an *Action Plan* with achievable time frames for each activity—don't take on too much at once otherwise nothing gets done.
- You need to stay on top of the plan annually and with life changes. Use the *Annual Review Checklist*.
- Acknowledge successes and accomplishments so far.
- You'll be happier because you will have a much better chance of living a comfortable, balanced and meaningful life.

Keep Up the Good Work

Momentum is a great thing. Once you start to move, momentum helps to keep you moving in the right direction. Continue your progress with some of the following strategies:

Schedule an hour a month for your money
It really isn't very much time, but it can be the difference between staying focused and using your money to achieve your goals, and falling back into familiar, but not-so-fabulous habits. Use the time to review what you have learned, review your goals, look up investing information, or make sure you are sticking to your *Spending and Savings Plan*.

Find money buddies

You may find that you would like to talk to others about what you have learned. Sharing what you have learned helps you to continue to learn and keeps the information fresh in your mind. Consider mentoring others to use their money to live their best life—what better gift? And when you start asking your friends about their financial know-how, you might be surprised at what valuable information they have to share with you. Consider getting a group of friends together, who share your goal of taking control of their financial future. Just as it's easier to keep up with your exercise program if you have buddies who are counting on you to show up, it can be easier to keep on track financially if you have friends who understand and are there to encourage you.

Continue to learn

We know how challenging it can be to stay motivated and on track with your money. Be sure to visit Money Coaches Canada—moneycoachescanada.ca—and take advantage of the courses, events and resources to continue to grow your financial wisdom and confidence.

Stay in touch

As Money Coaches, we can help you feel more confident and at ease with your money. We're not here to judge but to educate, empower and motivate you to take control of your financial future.

Drop us a line to let us know how you are doing. Or stay connected to us through our websites, Facebook, Twitter, newsletters, special events and other workshops. When you need it, our Money Coaches are available for one-on-one financial coaching and retirement planning for individuals, couples and entrepreneurs.

BOTTOM LINE, we are here to continue to support you to stay on track with your plan in any way we can.

My will shall shape the future. Whether I fail or succeed
shall be no man's doing but my own.
I am the force; I can clear any obstacle before me or I can be
lost in the maze.
My choice; my responsibility; win or lose, only I hold the
key to my destiny.

ELAINE MAXWELL

RESOURCES

Annual Tax and Financial Updates, Downloadable Workbook and Calculators in UNSTUCK are Available on our Website: moneycoachescanada.ca under Resources

Worksheets Included in Workbook

CHAPTER 6—Getting What You Really Want
- Dreams Page—If Money Wasn't an Issue, What Would You Do?
- Your Life and Financial Goals

CHAPTER 7—Your Financial Starting Point
- Details for Your Net Worth Statement
- Net Worth Statement
- Spending and Savings Plan

CHAPTER 8—On Track Money Management
- Annual or Lump Sum Expenses Worksheet

CHAPTER 11—Don't Give Up on Retirement Yet
- If Money Wasn't an Issue, What Would You Do?
- My Retirement Goals
- Retirement Lifestyle Expenses

CHAPTER 14—Just Do It
- Financial Plan Checklist
- Action Plan
- My Annual Review Checklist

Calculators Available on Website

CHAPTER 9—Debt: The Good, the Bad and the Ugly
· Debt-Free Calculator

CHAPTER 11—Don't Give Up on Retirement Yet
· Financial Freedom Calculator

RECOMMENDED READING

*The Beginner's Guide to Saving and Investing for Canadi-
ans* by Krystal Yee, Jim Yih, Ram Balakrishnan, Frugal
Trader and Glenn Cooke

Debt-Free Forever by Gail Vaz-Oxlade

*The Financially Empowered Woman: Everything You Really
Want to Know About Your Money* by Tracy Theemes

*The Millionaire Next Door: The Surprising Secrets of
America's Wealthy* by Thomas J. Stanley and William
D. Danko

Money, a Memoir: Women, Emotions, and Cash by Liz Perle

The Moolala Guide to Rockin' Your RRSP by Bruce Sellery

*Rob Carrick's Guide to What's Good, Bad and Downright
Awful in Canadian Investments Today* by Rob Carrick

*Seven Stages of Money Maturity: Understanding the Spirit
and Value of Money in Your Life* by George Kinder

Smart Couples Finish Rich by David Bach

*Start Late, Finish Rich: A No-Fail Plan for Achieving
Financial Freedom at Any Age* by David Bach

*The Soul of Money: Transforming Your Relationship with
Money and Life* by Lynne Twist

*Stop Over-Thinking Your Money!: The Five Simple Rules of
Financial Success* by Preet Banerjee

The Wealthy Barber Returns by David Chilton

Women & Money by Suze Orman

Your Money or Your Life by Vicki Robin, Joe Dominguez and
Monique Tilford

Money Coaches Canada
moneycoachescanada.ca

Women's Financial Learning Centre
womensfinanciallearning.ca

Canada Revenue Agency—tax information
cra-arc.gc.ca

Canada Revenue Agency—My Account
cra.gc.ca/myaccount

Canadian Couch Potato
canadiancouchpotato.com

The Canadian Institute of Financial Planners
cifps.ca

Credit Counselling Society (debt, bankruptcy and loan
calculators)
nomoredebts.org

Debtors Anonymous
debtorsanonymous.org

Equifax Canada Inc. (to get your credit report)
equifax.ca

Financial Advisors Association of Canada (find an advisor)
advocis.ca

Financial Consumer Agency of Canada
fcac-acfc.gc.ca

Globe Investor, Funds, The Globe and Mail (mutual fund
reviews, articles on mutual funds, etc)
globeinvestor.com

Investors Aid Co-operative of Canada
investors-aid.ca

MoneySense
moneysense.ca

MoneySense Approved Financial Advisors
moneysenseapproved.com

Service Canada
servicecanada.gc.ca

Strategis, Industry Canada (Canadian government
business and consumer site)
strategis.ic.gc.ca

TransUnion of Canada (to get your credit report)
transunion.ca

BLOGS WE LIKE
Money Coaches Canada Blog
moneycoachescanada.ca/blog

Canadian Finance Blog
canadianfinanceblog.com

Retire Happy Blog by Jim Yih
Retirehappyblog.ca

Squawkfox—Kerry K. Taylor
squawkfox.com

Steadyhand Blog—Cutting Through the Noise
steadyhand.com/blog

INDEX

Boldface page numbers indicate forms and worksheets.

A

accounts
  business chequing
    account, 106
  Main Chequing Account, **91**,
    101, 103-9, **174**
  Monthly Spending Account,
    91, 101-4, 106-7, **174**
  savings accounts, 103-4,
    107-14
  See also expenses; On Track
    Money Management
    System; Spending and
    Savings Plan; tax-free
    savings account (TFSA)
Action Plan, 222, **224**, 230
advice. *See* financial
  advisors; financial planners;
  investment advisors;
  money coaches
Annual or Lump Sum Expenses
  worksheet, **110**
Annual Review Checklist, 225,
  226, 230
annuities, 187-88

assets, 24, 80-81. *See also*
  investment; net worth;
  Net Worth Statement

B

bankruptcy, 52, 129,
  133-35, 235
brokers. *See* investment
  advisors
business income, 72-73, 93,
  106, **172**, 194, 200

C

Canada Pension Plan (CPP), 168,
  176-79, 181-82, 211
Canada Savings Bonds, 56,
  139, 142
capital gains, 143, 159, 161
capital losses, 143, 159
Care-Giving Plan of Action,
  45-47
cash flow
  business, 106
  managing, 24, 42, 51, 71-72,
    84, 88-**91**, 106, 192
  and retirement, 165, 178, 184

See also Spending and
Savings Plan; spending
patterns
charitable giving, 84, 88,
100, 208
chequing account. *See under*
accounts
children
education, 42-43, 100,
147, 203
money tips, 41-43
teens and money, 43-45
consumer culture, 9-10, 16,
30-32, 39-40
consumer proposal, 52, 134.
See also bankruptcy; debt
couples and money
attitudes towards debt,
36-39, 42
and children (*see* children)
communication about money,
10, 22, 28, 35
divorce, 22, 35, 193-94,
214-17
joint accounts, 38-39,
125-26, 210-12, 215
and overspending, 38-41
risk tolerance, 36
spousal RSP, 180-81
credit cards. *See under* debt
credit counseling, 51, 53,
134, 235
credit history, 25, 119-20,
129-30
credit rating, 129-31

D

debt, 8-9, 13, 18, 23, 31-32
and assets, 117
consolidation, 123, 134

credit card, 8-9, 23, 25,
116-19, 122-26, 128-33
culture, 8-9, 116, 118
and interest rates,
117-18, 122
and investing, 128
lifestyle, 30-32, 39-42, 116,
131-32
line of credit, 115, 117, 119
management, 23, 51-53, 65,
68, 80, 118-28, 133-35
(*see also* On Track Money
Management System;
Spending and Savings
Plan)
mortgage, 40, 117-18
retirement and, 170, 184
See also couples and
money; credit history;
overspending
Debt-Free Calculator, 126-27
Debt-Free Date, 123-27,
184, **226**
deductions, 42, 88, 158, 200
dividends, 143-44, 159, 161
divorce, 22, 35, 193-94, 214-17
donations, 84, 88, 100, 208
downsizing, 39-40, 185, 187
dreams, 19-21, 23, 37, 62-69,
64, 113, 170, 173, **224**. *See
also* financial plan; goals

E

emergency fund, 190-92.
See also insurance
emotional relationship to
money, 10-11, 13, 15-24,
27-34
fears, 3-4, 9-11, 24-29, 39,
117, 139, 157

happiness, 17-18, 20, 30-31
keeping up appearances,
   9-10, 30
parental influences, 10-11,
   20-22, 29-30
shame, 3, 9, 28-29, 117
See also dreams; goals
Employment Insurance (EI), 179
equities. *See* stocks
estate planning
   Advance Health Care
      Directive, 46, 212-13,
      227, 230
   and executor, 209-11
   Living Wills, 212-13
   power of attorney, 46, 211-12,
      215, 227, 230
   probate, 210-11
   Representation Agreement,
      212-13
   wills, 46, 81, 207-12, 215,
      223-24, 227, 230
exchange-traded funds (ETFs),
   149, 154-56
   vs. mutual funds, 154-55
expenses
   annual, 89-90, 101-4, 107-11,
      173-74
   Annual or Lump Sum
      Expenses worksheet, **110**
   lump sum, 89-90, 97, 101-4,
      107-13
   monthly, 38, 71-74, 89-90,
      101-7, 119, 173-74
   See also accounts; Spending
      and Savings Plan

F
financial advisors, 23, 36, 41,
   50-59, 100, 154, 168, 214-16

See also financial planners;
   money coaches
Financial Freedom Calculator,
   183
financial planners, 53, 56, 138,
   151, 153-54, 188. *See also*
   financial advisors; money
   coaches
financial plan, 24, 37-38, 61
Financial Plan Checklist, **223**
financial security, 19, 21, 36,
   85, 156-57, 198, 215-16
financial well-being, seven
   stages of, 12-15
fixed costs, 101, 104-5,
   109-10, 191

G
gifts, 87, 89-92, 104, 108-13,
   124-25
Goal-Centred Investment Plan,
   138-65, 229
   choosing account types,
      141-42
   management and review,
      163-65
   selecting investments, 149-63
   setting goals, 140-41
   understanding options,
      142-49
goals, 15, 62-63, 65-75
   conflicting, 71-74
   See also dreams; financial
      plan
Group Savings Plans, 42
Guaranteed Income Supplement
   (GIS), 161, 168, 179
Guaranteed Investment Certifi-
   cate (GIC), 55-56, 139, 142,
   145, 156, 159, 180-81

H

Home Buyers' Plan,
162–63
home ownership, 23, 72, 80,
161–63
as goal, 11, 42, 65, 67, 94,
112–13
and insurance, 189, 193, 197,
201–2, 204
in retirement, 46, **171**,
173, 185
saving for, 65, 85, 161–63
See also mortgage

I

illness/injury. *See* emergency
fund; insurance
income tax, 72, 185, 211
insurance, 192–206, 210,
227, 229
critical illness, 200–201
disability, 190, 198–200, 203
and divorce, 214–15
life, 194–97, 203, 210–11
long-term care, 201–2
and Spending and Savings
Plan, **91**–92, 101, 103–4,
108, **110**
interest
and debt, 25, 81, 117–23,
125–26, 128–29,
186–87
and investments, 142–43,
158–59
and savings, 104, 108–9,
113, 148, 156, 161, 192
and tax, 158–61 (*see also*
tax-free savings account
[TFSA])

investment
asset allocation, 144–49,
164–65, **226**, 227
asset classes: bonds, 54–56,
81, 139, 142–52, 156,
159–60, 164–65, 180–81;
cash, 54, 80–81, 142,
144–50, 156–65, 195–96,
215; stocks (*see* stocks)
leveraged, 128
non-registered, 141–42
portfolio, 17, 18–19, 54–56,
138, 140, 145, 154–58,
163–65
rebalancing, 164–65
registered, 141–42
risk tolerance, 36, 55, 128,
139–51, 154–58, 164–65,
176 (*see also* couples and
money)
and tax, 158–61
See also exchange-traded
funds (ETFs); financial
planners; investment
advisors; mutual funds;
Registered Retirement
Savings Plan (RSP); stocks;
tax-free savings account
(TFSA)
investment advisors, 49, 54–57,
138, 151, 155, 197
investment counselors, 57
investment plan, 25, 229
choosing account types,
141–42
management and review,
163–65
selecting investments,
149–63

setting goals, 140–41
understanding options,
142–49

J

joint accounts, 38–39, 125–26,
210–12, 215

L

liabilities, 24, 80–81, 215.
See also net worth; Net
Worth Statement
line of credit
about, 119
and debt, 42, 115, 117,
121–23, 125
and expenses, 108
as liability, 80, 81
paying off, 71, 184
loans, 105, 116–23, 129–30, 134
car, 116–17, 194
consolidation (see under
debt)
family, 81
personal, 80–81, 194
RSP, 187
student, 73, 80–81
See also line of credit

M

marriage, 41, 214–16, 225.
See also couples and money
maternity leave, 42, 73–74
media influences, 28. See also
consumer culture; debt:
culture
men and money, 10, 28,
39–41
money coaches, 100, 134, 188

what they do, 3, 52–53, 55,
231–32
working with couples, 22, 36,
40–41
money and happiness.
See emotional relationship
to money
money market accounts, 142,
151, 153
money and relationships.
See couples and money
money and shame. See
emotional relationship
to money
mortgage
applying for, 81, 120, 129
and debt, 40, 80–81, 116–18,
129–30, 173
and insurance, 195–97,
203–4
paying off, 72, **172**,
184–86, 193
as regular expense, 38,
85–86, 89, 104–5, 214–15
mutual funds, 54–57, 149–55,
160, 162–65, 181
cash assets, 149
balanced funds, 150
diversification, 145, 150–51
dollar cost averaging, 150
vs. exchange-traded funds
(ETFS), 154–55
factory direct mutual funds,
153–54
load mutual funds, 153–54
management expense ratio
(MER), 152–54
management fees, 152–54
money market, 151

prospectus, 151
stock, 148-49
and tax, 159, 180

N

net worth
building, 14, 38
determining, 79-83
investing and, 58,
143-44, 155
prenuptial agreement
and, 216
reviewing, 98
Net Worth Statement, 24, 81,
82-83, 98, 215, **226**, 229

O

Old Age Security (OAS), *161,
168, 179, 182*
On Track Money Management
System, 125
accounts for, 101-2, 104
diagram, 103
FAQs and objections, 113-14
implementing, 105-12
See also accounts; Spending
and Savings Plan
open accounts. *See* investment
accounts
overdraft, 104-5, 107, 119
overspending, 9-10, 23-24,
30-31
analyzing, 84-86
avoiding, 131-32
couples and, 36, 38-40
eliminating, 96, 98, 102
See also cash flow; consumer
culture; couples and
money; debt; Spending
and Savings Plan;
spending patterns

P

parents
Care-Giving Plan of Action,
45-47
and childhood lessons about
money, 11, 20-22, 28-30
elderly, 45-47, 194
pensions
Canada Pension Plan,
168, 176-79, 181-82,
187, 211
death and, 210, **223**, 227
defined benefit plan, 175,
181-82
defined contribution plan,
175-76, 180, 182
Old Age Security, 161, 168,
179, 182
power of attorney, 46,
211-12, 215, 227, 230
private investment managers,
57

R

real estate, 145, 161-63, 208,
210, 212, 215
Real Estate Investment Trust
(REIT), 161
Registered Education Savings
Plan (RESP), 67
Registered Retirement Savings
Plan (RSP), 210, 215, 227
borrowing for contributions,
187
as fixed expense, 105
and Home Buyers' Plan,
162-63,
as part of saving for retirement, 67, 71-72, 80-81,
141-42, 145-46,
spousal, 180-81

and tax, 158, 180, 185
and tax-free savings
  accounts, 160, 185–86
whether to invest in, 185–87
See also Guaranteed Income
  Supplement (GIS);
  pensions
relationships and money. *See*
  money and relationships
retail therapy, 131
retirement, 167–88
and debt, 170, 184
early, 17, 177–78
estimating income, 181–82
gap management, 183–84
goals, 169–72
plan, 25, 167–70
saving for, 71–72, 173,
  183–84, 187–88
worksheets, **171, 172**
Retirement Income Fund (RIF),
  54, 141–42, 158, 180–81
Retirement Lifestyle Expenses
  worksheet, 173, **174**, 183
risk tolerance. *See under*
  investment

S

saving. *See* accounts; On Track
  Money Management System;
  Spending and Savings Plan;
  tax-free savings account
  (TFSA)
self-employment
  and business accounts, 106
  and disability insurance, 190,
    198–200
  and paying yourself holiday
    pay, 106, 112
  and paying yourself a salary,
    88–89, 106

Spending and Savings Plan
  benefits of, 25, 84–87,
    92–93, 126
  information for, 87–90
  and saving for retirement,
    173
  setting up, 89–98, 190–91,
    205, 215
  using accounts, 105–8
  See also accounts; cash
    flow; On Track Money
    Management System;
    overspending; spending
    patterns
Spending and Savings Plan
  worksheet, 86, **91**
spending patterns, 29, 65, 79,
  86, 92, 120–21
spousal RSPs, 180–81
stocks
  about, 143
  asset allocation, 144–49,
    164–65
  capital gains, 159
  investing in, 54–58
  portfolio, 18–19
  and retirement, 165,
    180–81, 184
  and risk tolerance, 139
  See also investment
student loans, 73, 80–81, 122

T

tax
  capital gains, 143, 159, 161
  capital losses, 143, 159
  deductions, 42–43, 88
  and disability insurance,
    199–200
  and divorce, 215
  and estate planning, 207, 211

and investments, 157–61,
180, 185–87
and life insurance, 194–97
and pensions, 179–81
property tax expenses, 108
and RSPs, 185–87
tax-free savings account (TFSA),
141–42, 159–61, 181, 187
travel
in retirement, 173, 177
saving for, 38, 43–44,
86–87, 90, 95–97, 102–3,
112–14, 125

U
unemployment. *See* emergency
fund; insurance

V
vehicles. *See* expenses; fixed
costs; loans: car

W
wills. *See under* estate planning
women and money, 10, 22,
28, 39–41, 115, 137,
197, 231
worksheets
Action Plan, **224**
Annual or Lump Sum
Expenses, **110**
Annual Review Checklist,
226
dreams, **64**
Financial Plan Checklist, **223**
life and financial goals, **69**
Net Worth Statement, **82, 83**
retirement dreams, **171**
retirement goals, **172**
Retirement Lifestyle
Expenses, **174**
Spending and Savings
Plan, **91**

KARIN MIZGALA, MBA, CFP

Karin's life and career is based on a simple truth—life is not meant to be a struggle—it is here to be enjoyed. Her work as a financial educator is dedicated to helping individuals, families, and companies discover the transformative power of money so anyone can live the life they truly want.

Karin is a Certified Financial Planner with an MBA and a degree in Psychology. She has more than 25 years' experience in the financial services industry on Bay Street and in Vancouver. She has worked as a financial planner, bank manager, investment advisor, financial educator and life skills counselor.

Karin, and her husband Wayne, work from their homebase on Salt Spring Island. They practice meditation, love road trips, do a little gardening and enjoy life—she is grateful for it all.

SHEILA WALKINGTON, BBA, CFP

Sheila believes that people deserve to be happy. She is passionate about helping them take control of their money and freeing themselves of debt so they can live their dreams.

Sheila is a Certified Financial Planner with more than 20 years of experience in the banking and financial industry. When she started her financial planning career, no one was teaching the basics of money management. People would ask her, "Is there a book I can read? Can my bank help me?" The answer for Sheila was simple but bold: she would set out to revolutionize the world of financial planning. In 2004, CBC interviewed her as one of the first money coaches in Canada.

Sheila lives in Vancouver with her husband David. She enjoys yoga, playing hockey, and travelling.

KARIN AND SHEILA are both respected keynote speakers who speak to organizations, companies and media across Canada. They love to share their unique blend of inspiration and practicality that allows people to take control of their money and transform their lives.

Printed in the USA
CPSIA information can be obtained
at www.ICGtesting.com
JSHW021411220923
48800JS00005B/137